Shropshire
Railways

Shropshire Railways

GEOFF CRYER

THE CROWOOD PRESS

First published in 2014 by
The Crowood Press Ltd
Ramsbury, Marlborough
Wiltshire SN8 2HR

www.crowood.com

British Library Cataloguing-in-Publication Data
A catalogue record for this book is available from the British Library.

ISBN 978 1 84797 691 8

FRONTISPIECE: 46229 *Duchess of Hamilton* stands in the loop beside the
main line at Crewe Bank, Shrewsbury, after working in with a Welsh
Marches Pullman on 31 October 1982. Preserved steam locomotives
were able to take water here, courtesy of the local fire service.

Typeset by Bookcraft Ltd, Stroud, Gloucestershire
Printed and bound in Singapore by Craft Print International Ltd

Contents

Acknowledgements

This book would not have been possible without the assistance and support of many people. My thanks to everyone who has helped in any way, but especially Russell Mulford and Berwyn Stevens for access to their wonderful photographic collections, Dave Giddins for access to his archives, and Steve Price for checking the draft text (any mistakes remaining are the author's, not his) and for his photographs.

Thank you to Jamie Green, Charles Powell and Rob Weston for their help with 'Shropshire Railwaymen', and to the following for supply of photographs: John Powell at the Ironbridge Gorge Museum; David Postle at Kidderminster Railway Museum; the Industrial Railway Society; the Shropshire Railway Society; the Shrewsbury Railway Heritage Trust; John Chalcraft (RailPhotoprints.co.uk); Phil Darlaston; Robert Darlaston; Mark Norton; Bernard Stokes; Rob Smout; and Rob Weston. All uncredited photographs were taken by the author.

Lastly, thank you to Richard Fairhurst for kindly allowing me to use his excellent 'New Adlestrop Railway Atlas' as a basis for the maps – and to anyone else whom I may have forgotten.

Introduction

Four Hundred Years of Railways

Mention the county of Shropshire in conversation in other parts of the country and the outcome will too often be a blank look, a polite smile perhaps. Shropshire? Where's that? For some, Shropshire is that part of England which must be passed through to get to North Wales. Lacking the more spectacular scenery of its neighbour, the landlocked border county nevertheless has its attractions.

Shrewsbury, the county town, is one of Britain's finest medieval boroughs, with splendid streets of half-timbered buildings. The town centre is neatly contained within a loop of the River Severn. Barely a quarter-mile (400m) across the neck, the very pleasant walk across that neck and around the river bank, inside the loop, is about 2 miles (3km). In times when proximity to the Welsh border meant uncertainty, the loop made a natural defence for the town; the castle, straddling the neck, completed the defences.

Immediately beneath the castle walls lies Shrewsbury's substantial and attractive railway station. Despite losing its overall roof in the early

The magnificent stone frontage of Shrewsbury station, as seen from the Dana footpath on Sunday, 30 June 2013. The line to Hereford was closed for engineering work (lowering the track under a number of bridges along the line, to enable trains carrying large containers to use the route), hence the substitute road coaches in the forecourt.

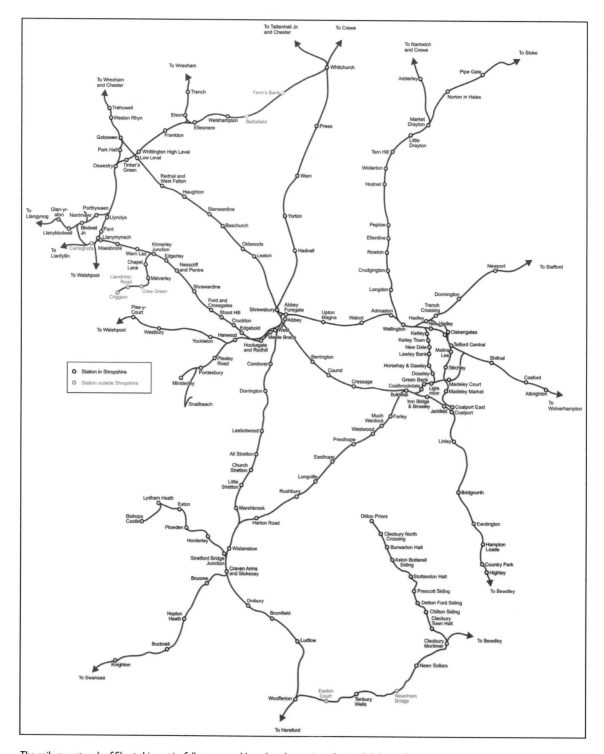

The railway network of Shropshire, at its fullest extent. Note that the stations depicted did not all exist concurrently.

1960s, it is very much a 'traditional' large station, whose stone main building has been grade II listed since 1969. Shrewsbury's signalling, though simplified over the years, remains primarily mechanical, with an interesting mix of upper- and lower-quadrant signals. Severn Bridge Junction signal box, also grade II listed, has been since 2008 the world's largest surviving mechanical signal box and is likely to remain so for several more years.

The Shropshire Hills Area of Outstanding Natural Beauty is mostly contained within a much greater loop of the Severn, which flows northeast through Newtown and Welshpool, enters Shropshire near Melverley, meanders eastwards through Shrewsbury, ever more southwards from Ironbridge to Bridgnorth, and on down towards Worcester. A.E. Housman's 'blue remembered hills' are well worth visiting. Church Stretton is one of a number of places which, in Victorian times, bore the accolade 'Little Switzerland'. An exaggeration, of course, but standing on the platform at Church Stretton station and gazing around, it can be hard to believe this is part of the English Midlands. Church Stretton marks the summit of the Hereford line's long climb southwards from the county town, a notable challenge for locomotive crews in steam days. A plaque on the platform notes its height – 613ft (187m) above sea level – and its longitude. Church Stretton's true noon follows eleven minutes and twelve seconds after Greenwich, although the coming of the railways would mean an end to 'local time'.

The railway from Welshpool to Shrewsbury runs little more than a couple of miles south of the river; the Severn Valley line followed the river downstream from the county town. North of the river lies a gentler landscape, more arable with fewer sheep. Radiating through that country are the lines from Shrewsbury to Chester, Crewe and Wolverhampton.

Shropshire's attractive old market towns deserve exploration, although today significantly fewer are served by the railway. Whitchurch, Wem and Wellington can still be visited by rail, but Market

Trevithick's 1808 Catch Me Who Can *was built at the Hazeldine foundry in Bridgnorth – it was the world's first railway locomotive to haul fare-paying passengers, on a circular track in London. This replica was also built in Bridgnorth, 200 years later. Not quite complete, the loco was on blocks, in steam and rotating its wheels slowly in June 2011.*

Drayton, Oswestry and Bridgnorth are no longer on the national network. It is, however, towns such as Bridgnorth and Ironbridge that have, in relatively recent years, really helped to put the county on the map.

Bridgnorth was a popular destination for tourists and day-trippers long before the Severn Valley Railway (SVR) began running steam trains in 1970. Today, the SVR is recognized not only as a premier heritage railway, but also as a major tourist attraction on a national level. Almost forgotten until recently was Bridgnorth's role in early steam locomotive construction – Richard Trevithick's 1808 *Catch Me Who Can*, which pulled the world's first steam-hauled passenger train, was built at Hazeldine's foundry in Bridgnorth's Low Town.

When the Bridgnorth Cliff Railway opened in 1892, it used the water-balance method, but was later converted to electric power. It connects the Low Town with the High Town, saving pedestrians from a long flight of steps; 21 April 2013.

Bridgnorth also has what claims to be 'England's oldest and steepest inland electric funicular railway'. Similar to seaside funiculars, it is still in operation more than 120 years after its construction.

The Ironbridge Gorge was declared a World Heritage Site in 1986, in recognition of the area's role in the Industrial Revolution. The Ironbridge Gorge Museum is a substantial and rewarding tourist destination for visitors. Notwithstanding Abraham Darby's major contribution to industrial history – the first use of coke in iron-making at the Coalbrookdale works – Ironbridge can claim a number of railway 'firsts', including the casting of the world's first iron rails and the building of the world's first steam railway locomotive in 1802. Two hundred years earlier, across the River

This working replica of Trevithick's 1802 Coalbrookdale locomotive was completed in 1990 by apprentices at GKN Sankey's works in Hadley, Telford. It is regularly demonstrated in steam for visitors to Blists Hill Victorian Town; 30 July 2009.

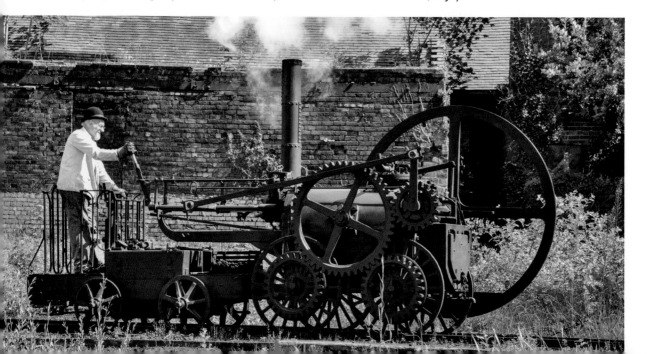

Severn in nearby Broseley, a wooden wagonway is known to have existed in 1605. It is possible that it predated the Wollaton Wagonway, the world's first documented railway, which was completed just west of Nottingham in 1604. A significant mileage of pre-railway age wagonways or tramways existed in Shropshire when conventional railways came to the county in the mid-nineteenth century.

Given this place in early railway history, it is ironic that Shrewsbury was the second to last English county town to be connected to the growing national network of conventional railways. Thomas Telford's Holyhead road passed through the county and, in the same way, the earliest main-line schemes to be planned for Shropshire would have passed through en route to the Welsh coast for the Irish Sea traffic. In the event, none of those schemes came to fruition – Shropshire's railways eventually came as lines to serve Shrewsbury. At the time of writing it has, once again, no through service to London. Nor are there any electrified railways in the county.

Shropshire's railway history may appear contradictory; it is certainly quirky, particularly in geographical terms. The River Teme threads the county's southern border country, almost from its source in the Welsh Kerry Forest until it leaves the county to the east of Worcestershire's Tenbury Wells. Tenbury's railway station, on the north side of the Teme, was in Shropshire. Until 1961, one could travel by rail from Tenbury to Knighton, about 25 miles (40km) upstream. It could take a couple of hours or more, with two changes of trains. Knighton is in Wales, but its railway station, like Tenbury's, is on the north bank of the Teme, in Shropshire, England.

Geographically, the biggest Welsh railway was the Cambrian Railways (always plural) Company, whose headquarters and substantial railway works were in Oswestry, Shropshire. Today, other than the Wolverhampton line's stations and local trains, all of this English county's passenger train services and stations are provided and managed by Arriva Trains Wales.

Shropshire's involvement with the main-line railways began several years before it had any of its own – this tube for Brunel's ill-fated atmospheric railways, seen at the National Railway Museum (NRM), York, in July 1984, was cast at Coalbrookdale in the early 1840s.

Minor Lines

Shropshire was once blessed with a wealth of minor railways, each with its idiosyncrasies. The Bishop's Castle Railway opened (unofficially) in 1865 and (officially) in 1866. The only part constructed of an intended through route, it ran in the hands of the Official Receiver from the end of that year until its inevitable closure in 1935.

The grandiose Potteries, Shrewsbury and North Wales Railway scheme also only partially achieved its ambitions. Opening in 1866, it was closed completely fourteen years later. Reopened by Colonel Stephens as the Shropshire and Montgomeryshire Railway (S&M) in 1911, it was moribund when it became a World War II military railway, which survived until 1960.

The 'Potts' extension from Llanymynech to Nantmawr passed into Cambrian hands, and the last mile or so remains in existence, in the hands of preservationists. It connects with a remnant of another minor railway – the Tanat Valley. The first 8 miles (13km) of the 20-mile (32km) branch, which ultimately became part of the national network, were in Shropshire.

The Snailbeach railway, which also became part of the Colonel Stephens empire, was a 2ft 4in (711mm) gauge line opened in 1877 to provide lead mines at Snailbeach with an outlet to the main lines. In its last years, with no usable locomotives, a farm tractor, wheels straddling the rails, was used to haul and shunt its wagons.

The Cleobury Mortimer and Ditton Priors Light Railway survived until 1965. Like the S&M, World War II extended its life. Despite its distance from the sea, it was operated in its last years by the Admiralty.

Industrial Railways

Despite its generally rural nature, Shropshire had some significance in the field of industrial railways. Its mines had railways and most used locomotives. Ifton Colliery, in the north-western corner of the county, was at one time Shropshire's biggest mine; its last was Telford's Granville Colliery, which closed in 1979. Granville's railway was the last surviving part of the Lilleshall Company's private railway, which once served mines, a steel works, brick works and the company's engineering works at St George's. The company was, for a time, a builder of steam locomotives, though sadly none has survived into preservation. The locomotive *Peter*, a static exhibit at Blists Hill, first worked at Kinlet Colliery, one of several in the south-east of the county, around Highley.

Ironbridge Power Station had its own steam locomotives, two of which are preserved. *Lewisham,* from Allscott sugar factory, also escaped the scrap man. The army depot at Donnington, Telford, had its own internal railway system. Although no longer using locomotives, its rail connection, lifted in 1989, was reopened twenty years later to serve the depot and a general freight terminal nearby.

Shrewsbury was a significant builder of industrial locomotives. Sentinel's economical little vertical-boilered machines were turned out until 1958, then, taken over by Rolls-Royce, the business made a very successful transition to diesel power. Later sold as Rolls-Royce locomotives, Shrewsbury-built diesel shunting locomotives were widely used in industry.

The subject of railways in Shropshire is both broad and deep. The topics within each chapter would themselves be worth a substantial book, many of which have been published, and many topics have been tackled more than once. This book cannot hope to encompass the depth of those works, but in exploring the breadth of the subject, will perhaps encourage the reader to further study of those areas that particularly catch the imagination – for a good imagination is a valuable asset where much of the county's railway interest is concerned. Much has gone, and redevelopment has in some cases removed all traces of what was once there, especially within the bounds of Telford.* The appended bibliography may provide a useful starting point for further reading.

---

* The Borough of Telford and Wrekin is a unitary authority, historically and geographically located within Shropshire.

CHAPTER I

The Pre-Railway Age

Earliest Times

Mining for coal in East Shropshire can be traced back at least as far as the thirteenth century, possibly to Roman times. The numerous bell pits and adits were already a feature of the area when the first tentative steps to railway construction were taken. In 1605, a wooden railway carrying coal from Broseley, via Birch Batch* to the River Severn at the Calcutts, was the subject of a dispute between James Clifford, lord of the manor, and his tenants Messrs Wilcox and Wells, who had built the line.

It is not certain when, exactly, the line was constructed. In 1604, the Wollaton Wagonway opened in Nottinghamshire, to carry coal from mines at Strelley to Wollaton, mostly for onwards movement by road to the River Trent. The Wollaton line is generally regarded as the first overland true railway in the world (more primitive wagonways in mines used plain wheels on boards, with pins and slots for guidance). Recently, there have been suggestions that the Broseley line may already have been in existence when the Nottinghamshire line opened

– might Shropshire be the home of the world's first railway?

Without further documentary evidence, that claim may have to remain unfounded. Huntingdon Beaumont, who built the Wollaton line, went on to develop primitive railways in Northumberland, where a horse would haul a single large chaldron

Early days at Blists Hill: the 'Open Air Museum' opened in 1973. In June of that year, wagons stand on the plateway beside Andrew Barclay-built Peter, *whose career began at Kinlet Colliery in the south of the county.*

---

* A 'batch' (or beach, as in Snailbeach) in Shropshire is a valley.

wagon. The practice that developed in Shropshire was to haul several small wagons, coupled together – if not the first railway, then perhaps the first trains.

The Broseley dispute, heard in the Court of the Star Chamber, related to 'A very artificialle Engine or Instrument of Timber ... [consisting of] ... fframes and Rayles.' Today, the locomotive is the 'engine', but that description of the railway lives on in local memories. The oldest residents of Coalbrookdale may remember the 'jenny' or 'jinnie' rails', which ran down the dale into the twentieth century. Several 'jenny wagons' have survived to be preserved locally.

Within a year or two of the dispute mentioned above, James Clifford had built his own (shorter) line from mines near Calcutts to the Severn and such railways soon became a feature of local mining. Parts of the original route may have been incorporated into the later line known as the 'Jackfield Rails', which also carried coal down to the river at the Calcutts.

In the early years of the eighteenth century, another coal-carrying line was constructed nearby, utilizing the valley of Tarbatch Dingle to descend eastwards to the Severn. In 1757, a westward extension connected the New Willey furnaces to the river, along a line of rails now extending almost 2.5 miles (4km). A junior partner in the furnaces was the notable 'Iron-Mad' John Wilkinson, who in 1787 launched the world's first iron boat from Willey Wharf, the riverside terminus of the line. Much to the amazement of onlookers, it floated.

Just south of the Tarbatch line, the 1780 Caughley Railway connected to the Severn at Bagley's Rough. Again, fragments of its route can be traced in the vicinity of Caughley Farm and Inett. West of Broseley, the Benthall Rails ran from quarries on Benthall Edge, where a small brick arch and a cutting may be remnants. A branch of this line (perhaps it was the main line) may have provided the New Willey furnaces with an alternative link to the river.

Clearly, there was much early railway activity south of the river during the 250 years prior to the coming of the main lines. Some of their routes (or parts thereof) can be proved, but some are conjectural. The first edition of the Ordnance Survey 1in map shows several 'Rail Roads', south of the river, including the Tarbatch line and the Benthall Rails, plus a line from quarries on Gleedon Hill, near Much Wenlock, to a wharf beside the Severn near Buildwas Park.

North of the Severn

North of the river, on the same map, many more 'Rail Roads' are marked, along with the newly constructed main-line railways. (There is a gap between Lightmoor and Buildwas Junction – that stretch of the Wellington to Craven Arms railway had yet to be built.) By the time the OS map was surveyed, many of the wagonways had been and gone. To catalogue them all would be a substantial task, but it is worth outlining the routes of some of the more extensive.

The Coalbrookdale wagonways were perhaps the most extensive and part of the network was still in use into the 1930s. The schematic (and simplified) map shows the lines running from the warehouse (now home to the Museum of the Gorge) and wharves on the Severn near Ironbridge, up Coalbrookdale (via Darby's ironworks) to Lightmoor furnaces and brickworks, on via the furnaces at Dawley to Horsehay ironworks, to end at Lawley.

The Madeley Wood system linked Bedlam furnaces, beside the Severn near Ironbridge, with Blists Hill ironworks, the company's mines and other operations. A high wrought iron bridge was built in 1872 to carry the line across the dingle from Blists Hill; a steep incline then took the line up past the All Nations Inn towards Madeley and the Meadow Pit Colliery. Beyond, the rails extended to Styches Colliery and back down to Bedlam, with a branch to brick and tile works above Ironbridge. The grade II listed Lee Dingle Bridge at Blists Hill remains a significant feature of the locality and the incline, now a public footpath, can be walked today.

Further north, early lines predated the railway developed by the Lilleshall Company and some

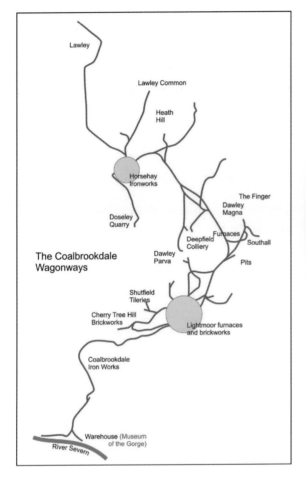

The Coalbrookdale Wagonways

ABOVE: An early photograph showing a Shropshire 'train' – three wagons loaded with limestone stand on the plateway beside New Pool, Coalbrookdale. IRONBRIDGE GORGE MUSEUM TRUST

LEFT: Of the many plateways in eastern Shropshire, the Coalbrookdale network was possibly the most extensive. Parts of the route depicted are conjectural and it may have extended further north than shown.

remained for a number of years as feeders to their successor.

The wagonways developed over the years. Like modern railways, the earliest used flanged wheels, but wheels and rails were of wood. As iron-making and associated trades developed and iron became cheaper, wood was gradually replaced. The first iron wheels were used on the wagonway between Little Wenlock and Strethill in 1729. Cheaper to make, their disadvantage was that they wore the rails more quickly. Replaceable strips of hardwood – beech or plane and later iron – were fitted on the top surface of oak (and later softwood) rails. Track of this kind was known as 'double way' (not the same as 'double track'). Typically, the sleepers and the primary rails were buried in the ballast, making

a suitable surface for the horses – only the top rail would be visible.

In 1767, at Coalbrookdale, whole rails were cast for the first time; these were rapidly adopted as the new standard. South of the river, John Wilkinson was another early user of iron rails, again to replace wood on tramways in the Tarbach and Benthall areas. Cast deeper in the middle than at either end, the shape led to their description as 'fishbelly' rails.

A reversal of early railway practice came about with the development of the plateway, whose flanged or L-shaped rails enabled the use of plain wheels. First used in Shropshire on the Ketley Canal's inclined plane, which was constructed in 1788, they came to the Coalbrookdale area around the beginning of the nineteenth century. Whilst the

The Coalbrookdale plateway ran to the Severn near Ironbridge – its former warehouse is now the Museum of the River. A plateway wagon stands on the trough-type rails used where the L-shaped rail might cause problems. Photograph taken in June 2013.

Iron could also be used for the sleepers of these plateways. They were cast with cut-outs for the rails, which could then be secured in place with wooden pegs. Rails were typically around 5ft–5ft 6in (1,500–1,700mm) in length, though the gauge used by the plateways could vary; 28in (710mm) was common and was in effect the wagonway 'standard gauge' within Coalbrookdale works.

North-West Shropshire

East Shropshire was not the only area to make use of early railways. On the western side of the county, where the border hills begin to rise, minerals have been exploited over a long period. Copper, lead, zinc and silver were extracted from Llanymynech Ogof, the mine on Llanymynech Hill, as long ago as the Bronze Age; the mine was last worked in the nineteenth century. More obvious to the casual visitor is the evidence of stone quarrying, again on Llanymynech Hill, and in the hills just to the north at Porthywaen, Blodwell, Whitehaven, Llynclys and Nantmawr. Despite their names, the quarries are, or were, mostly in Shropshire. The mine on Llanymynech Hill was in Wales (in the middle of what is now Llanymynech golf course), surrounded on three sides by Shropshire. Llanymynech itself neatly straddles the border – such is the nature of the border country.

flange was generally on the inside, double-flanged or channel-shaped rails were used for crossings and similar – such rails can be seen today, in situ at the riverside warehouse in Ironbridge.

Built around 1759, this bridge at Newdale carried the plateway between Horsehay and Ketley and is a rare survivor from those early days; 27 February 2013.

In this 1920s view looking towards the Severn warehouse (out of sight a little way along the road), are the disused remains of the 'jinnie rails' at Dale End, Coalbrookdale. The building on the left is in use today as a shop, but the buildings in the middle of the picture have long since gone. IRONBRIDGE GORGE MUSEUM TRUST

In 1796, the Llanymynech branch of the Ellesmere Canal opened for traffic, tapping the output of the quarries and lime kilns. Means of transporting goods to the canal were now required. At Llanymynech, inclined planes and associated tramways were constructed from the 'Welsh Quarry' and the 'English Quarry' in 1806 and 1810 respectively, to lime kilns near the canal. A large Hoffman kiln was built here around 1900; nevertheless, quarrying and lime-burning ended in 1914. The kiln remains, within the care of Shropshire County Council, as part of the Llanymynech Heritage Area.

The narrow-gauge Crickheath Tramway opened in the 1820s, connecting Porthywaen quarries to a wharf on the canal. It closed in 1913, but traces remain, in particular the abutments of the bridge built to carry the tramway over the Cambrian Railways. These are on the site of the new Llynclys station opened by the Cambrian Railways Trust at the northern end of its short line to Pant and preservation of their remains seems assured. At Crickheath Wharf on the canal, the Waterway Recovery Group is restoring the tramway wharf area.

The Morda Tramway operated between 1813 and 1879, connecting Coed-y-Go Pit, near Morda, to Gronwen Wharf on the canal. When the Drill Colliery opened in 1836, it too was connected to the tramway and the tramway was upgraded for heavier loads. Later, railway engineer Thomas Savin constructed a narrow-gauge railway to connect Coed-y-Go to the Cambrian Railways near Whitehaven. Its life was short – it had gone by the time the tramway ceased operations.

In the extreme north-west of the county, the Quinta Tramway connected mines to the Shropshire Canal. For a short time, it also connected to the Glyn Valley Tramway. The latter, a roadside tramway, was for most of its life operated by steam tram engines, running from the (mostly) slate workings higher up the valley to Chirk station, on the Shrewsbury and Chester line, and ran entirely within Wales. However, when built, it connected not to the railway, but to the Shropshire Canal, and it did so within Shropshire.

The End of an Era

The coming of the main-line railways marked the end of an era for the plateways, though perhaps not quite as rapidly as might be expected. The earliest wagonways had been constructed to provide links to the river; when the canals came, new plateways were developed as feeders. When the railways opened, plateways were built or extended to link to those lines for much the same reason. Their demise was gradual, lines closing or falling into disuse as the older mines and works closed, or when other means of transport made them redundant. The last use of the former Coalbrookdale network was as late as October 1932, when the section between Lightmoor and the Shutfield tile works closed.

Remnants of the plateways can still be seen in the area. The rails at the riverside warehouse are easily accessible, as are those within the Blists Hill Museum area. Some of the many public footpaths on either side of the Severn gorge follow the routes of these early railways, though today it may require a little imagination to see them for what they were.

CHAPTER 2

The Coming of the Main Lines

'Firsts' are rarely easy to define. The 1825 Stockton and Darlington was not the first railway, but as the first passenger-carrying railway financed by public subscription, its opening in 1825 is generally taken to mark the beginning of railways as we know them.

Over the following years, tentatively at first, the network grew and developed. A major milestone was the opening of the Liverpool and Manchester in 1830 (first double-track line, with timetabled services, using steam locomotives). The L&M was absorbed by the Grand Junction Railway in 1845, which the following year merged with the London and Birmingham and the Manchester and Birmingham to form the London and North Western Railway (LNWR), which would become a major player in Shropshire. By this date, there were railways operating in most parts of England and some lines had opened in Scotland and Wales. Not in Shropshire, however. Although the geographically limited network of primitive plateways and wagonways was thriving, conventional railways did not reach Shropshire until 1848.

The earliest plans involving Shropshire had been for railways with wider horizons. Many early schemes were aimed at the Welsh coast for the Irish Sea traffic. Such unlikely places as Porthmadog and Porth Dinlleyn were identified as possible major ports. The railways to serve them would have (incidentally) passed through Shropshire – but would also have had to pass through the Welsh mountains. Even when the main lines were mostly in place, schemes were still being promoted, such as the Potteries, Shrewsbury and North Wales Railway, and the Manchester and Milford Haven. Their routes would have crossed in Shropshire. Neil Rhodes, in his book *Trains on the Border – The Railways of Llanymynech and Pant* speculates on what might have been: Llanymynech could have been the Crewe of the Welsh borders.

The Shrewsbury and Chester opened in 1848. The following year, when the Shrewsbury and Birmingham opened to Wolverhampton, and the

These old documents date from the early days of Shropshire's railways: the Shrewsbury and Birmingham; Shrewsbury and Chester; Shrewsbury and Hereford; Great Western; and London and North Western railways are all represented here. DAVE GIDDINS COLLECTION

Shropshire Union opened to Stafford, more direct connections to London became possible. The line south to Hereford opened in 1853, and the Shrewsbury to Crewe line followed in 1858. The latter was opened by the LNWR, which by now incorporated the Shropshire Union. Meanwhile, the railways to Chester and Wolverhampton had become part of the Great Western Railway (GWR) and the pattern was set for the future ownership of most of Shropshire's railways. Some lines would be purely GWR, some purely LNWR, but joint ownership of the railway between Shrewsbury and Wellington had established a practice that would continue. Ultimately, the main line from Shrewsbury to Hereford and its branches to Tenbury Wells and Clee Hill, the Shrewsbury to Buttington (and thence Welshpool) railway and the Minsterley branch all formed part of the GWR and LNWR joint network. Apart from minor railways, other companies would only operate on the fringes of the county.

Railway Mania

Speculative investment 'bubbles' are neither new nor things of the past. The notorious South Sea Bubble peaked in 1720; its crash left many people much poorer. Isaac Newton lost £20,000 – a fortune in today's terms. Much more recently, the 'Dotcom' bubble peaked in March 2000. The 'Railway Mania' of the 1840s had some similarities, in that the huge temporary surge in the value of railway company shares became a self-perpetuating spiral. Speculators wanted to buy railway company shares because their prices were rising – but their prices were rising because speculators wanted to buy more and more of them. The mania peaked in 1845, when 248 railway bills were placed before Parliament.

Many people lost a great deal of money in the aftermath. Some schemes were entirely fraudulent, while others were not practical. Some were simply too ambitious for their potential traffic. But over 6,000 miles (9,700km) of railway were actually built, some of them in Shropshire. Some were entirely viable; others failed, often because of the inflated construction costs, but were then bought by the developing major railway companies, such as the Great Western and the London and North Western.

As befits its status as county town, the early development of Shropshire's railways focused on Shrewsbury. Four of the five lines that still radiate from the county town were promoted as the 'Shrewsbury and ... Railway'. The cross-county lines developed later.

The Shrewsbury and Chester Railway

The Denbighshire coalfield, centred on the area around Wrexham and Ruabon, extends southwards into Shropshire in the vicinity of St Martins. In 1844, to serve the mines, construction of the North Wales Mineral Railway (NWMR) began and by 1846 the area was connected to the growing national network.

When the Chester and Holyhead Act was passed in 1844, other early schemes for lines to the Welsh coast faded away. However, the promoters of the NWMR learned of plans by the London and Birmingham Railway for a Shropshire and Cheshire Railway, which would join the Holyhead line at Chester. Partly to thwart those ambitions, the NWMR's promoters submitted plans to Parliament for an extension to Shrewsbury, but they were rejected.

The Shrewsbury, Oswestry and Chester Junction Railway was then promoted independently and obtained its Act in 1845. The following year, it merged with the NWMR to become the Shrewsbury and Chester Railway. Construction completed, the line opened on 12 October 1848. Travelling from Chester via Wrexham, the line enters Shropshire on a fine stone viaduct across the Ceiriog valley, beside the earlier Llangollen canal aqueduct. The contractor for the railway's construction was Thomas Brassey, in partnership with Robert Stephenson and William Mackenzie. Brassey would later be involved with the Shrewsbury and Hereford, among others. Despite its original title, the route bypassed Oswestry, which would be served by a short branch line from Gobowen.

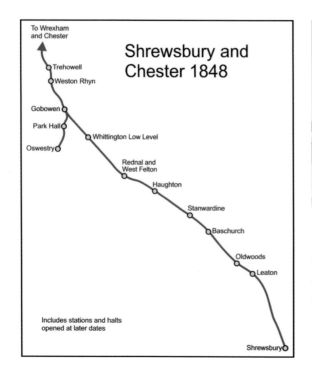

Shrewsbury and Chester 1848

To Wrexham and Chester

Trehowell
Weston Rhyn
Gobowen
Park Hall
Whittington Low Level
Oswestry
Rednal and West Felton
Haughton
Stanwardine
Baschurch
Oldwoods
Leaton
Shrewsbury

Includes stations and halts opened at later dates

Map of the Shrewsbury and Chester Railway.

The Italianate-style buildings at Gobowen station are grade II listed. Gobowen was relatively unimportant when the Shrewsbury and Chester line was built; the station's significance was that it served the branch to the much larger Oswestry; 19 February 2013.

The Shrewsbury and Chester Railway ran via Wrexham, in north-east Wales. 6201 Princess Elizabeth has just entered Shropshire; the rear of its train is still in Wales as it crosses Chirk viaduct with a 'steam special' on 12 June 1978. BERWYN STEVENS

Miles	Stations
0	Shrewsbury
3¾	Leaton
5½	Oldwoods Halt
7¾	Baschurch
9	Stanwardine Halt
11¾	Haughton Halt
13¼	Rednal and West Felton
16¼	Whittington Low Level
18	Gobowen
20	Weston Rhyn
20¼	Trehowell Halt
42½ (68km)	Chester

Miles	Stations
0	Gobowen
1¾	Park Hall Halt
2½ (4km)	Oswestry

All tables are based on early BR timetables, and include stations opened at later dates.

Closed

Cambrian Heritage Railways

Outside county

OFF THE RAILS

On 7 July 2012, a long and heavy coal train became derailed on the junction at the north end of Shrewsbury station. The train, running from Portbury, Avonmouth, to Fiddlers Ferry Power Station, was travelling at less than 15mph (24km/h) and remained upright. No one was hurt, but the track was damaged and the disruption to some passenger services was described as 'major travel chaos' in the local press. Journey times were extended by forty minutes on northbound trains between South Wales and Manchester, and those poor souls heading for Chester had to go by road coach. The train had been moved the following day and the track affected was soon repaired and back in use.

Britain's railways are, statistically, a very safe means of transport. The Rail Safety and Standards Board, in its *Annual Safety Performance Report 2011–2012*, reports just twelve fatalities in the last ten years, due to what it defines as 'train accidents' (not including fatalities at the platform edge, level crossings and so on). Between 1999 and 2008, more than 30,000 people were killed in road accidents in the UK – 870 in West Mercia (Shropshire, Herefordshire and Worcestershire) alone. One may wonder what the true significance of that coal train derailment was.

Throughout the period of public railways in Shropshire, there have been few fatalities – but there have been a small number of accidents that are worth a closer look and we will do so throughout this chapter.

Rednal 1865

On 7 June 1865, a heavy double-headed excursion train was travelling from Chester towards Shrewsbury. Just north of Rednal station, a permanent way gang was 'lifting and packing' the track, an operation that requires the sleepers to be raised slightly, in order to feed more ballast under them. Packing helps to ensure a smooth ride over rail joints, which are susceptible to the development of dips.

The driver of the leading engine, Anderson, did not appear to see a green warning flag on a pole, just over half a mile (800m) north of the work. The driver of the second engine saw it and blew his whistle, to no avail. Anderson shut off steam and applied the brakes when he saw the gang, far too late. A falling gradient, the weight of the train and inefficient brakes meant it was still travelling at almost full speed when it ran onto the raised rails. It became derailed, but remained upright until it struck points at Rednal station. The second engine then ploughed into it, followed by the leading coaches of the train, the first four of which were completely wrecked. Anderson, the second locomotive's fireman and eleven passengers were killed and thirty were injured.

The Shrewsbury and Birmingham Railway

Although the Shrewsbury and Chester was the county's first 'proper' railway, a more significant development, in many ways, was the opening of the Grand Junction Railway (GJR), more than ten years earlier in 1837. Arguably Britain's first arterial railway, it linked Birmingham, via Wolverhampton and Stafford, to Liverpool and Manchester. Crewe, a Cheshire village of fewer than 100 inhabitants, was chosen as a site for the company's engineering works. Over a ten-year period from 1849, three railways were opened that would ultimately link Shrewsbury with the GJR (which was now the LNWR), firstly at Wolverhampton and Stafford, then later at Crewe. The connection at Wolverhampton would be problematic, as the GJR's station was actually at Wednesfield Heath, about a mile to the east of the town centre.

The Shrewsbury and Birmingham Railway (S&B) never reached Birmingham. Planned in

Miles	Stations
0	Shrewsbury
3¾	Upton Magna
6¼	Walcot
8½	Admaston
10¼	Wellington
12	New Hadley Halt
13	Oakengates
14¼	Telford Central
17¼	Shifnal
20½	Cosford
22	Albrighton
29¾ (48km)	Wolverhampton Low Level
42¼	Birmingham Snow Hill
152¾ (246km)	Paddington

Closed

Outside county

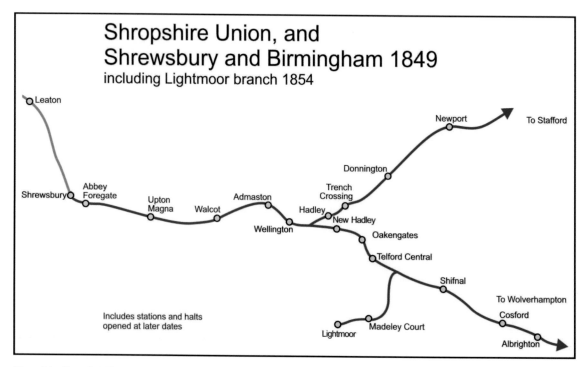

Map of the Shropshire Union and Shrewsbury and Birmingham railways.

On the Shrewsbury and Birmingham Railway, the ironwork for Oakengates Bridge was made by the Lilleshall Company. Photograph taken 4 June 2013.

in the tunnel, it could get no further; it opened through to Wolverhampton on 12 November of the same year. Remarkably, it would be another five years before through services would run over the S&B to London and those required changing trains, as the GWR had originally been built to broad gauge. It was not until 1880 that trains could run through to London, and that was by the 'Great Way Round' via Didcot. In 1910, the Oxford cut-off, from Aynho Junction to Paddington via High Wycombe, was opened, bringing Shrewsbury 19 miles (31km) nearer Paddington.

The Shropshire Union – Shrewsbury to Stafford

The Shropshire Union Railways and Canal Company (SUR&CC) came into existence as a result of an 1846 Act of Parliament. Primarily an amalgamation of the Ellesmere, the Chester and the Birmingham and Liverpool Junction canal companies, it also absorbed the Shrewsbury Canal; others, such as the Montgomery and the Shropshire Canal companies, would follow. They had begun to examine the possibility of converting their canals

1844 as a line running via Wolverhampton and Dudley, its Act, passed on 3 August 1846, authorized only the Shrewsbury to Wolverhampton section. Instead of its own line to Birmingham, it would have running powers over the Stour Valley line – the Birmingham, Wolverhampton and Dudley Railway, in which it would have a quarter share of the capital, was authorized the same day. The other quarter owners were the Stour Valley company itself, the Birmingham Canal Navigations (BCN) and the London and Birmingham Railway, which became part of the LNWR in 1846. The LNWR effectively gained control over the Stour Valley through arrangements with the BCN and it was the LNWR that began its construction in 1847.

On that busy day in Parliament, the Act authorizing the Shropshire Union Railway and its Shrewsbury to Stafford line was also passed. The S&B and the Shropshire Union would share construction and operation of the Shrewsbury to Wellington line, common to both railways. The ironwork for Belvidere Bridge, on the eastern edge of Shrewsbury, was cast at Coalbrookdale.

The railway opened from Shrewsbury as far as Oakengates on 1 June 1849 (the same day as the Shropshire Union to Stafford). With work ongoing

Miles	Stations
0	Shrewsbury
3¾	Upton Magna
6¼	Walcot
8¾	Admaston
10½	Wellington
11¾	Hadley
12½	Trench Crossing
14¼	Donnington
17¾	Newport
29¼ (47km)	Stafford

Closed

Outside county

Shropshire Union: an ex-LNWR 'coal tank' arrives at Newport station with a stopping train from Stafford in early BR days. W.H. SMITH COLLECTION/ KIDDERMINSTER RAILWAY MUSEUM

OFF THE RAILS: DONNINGTON, 1852

The Shropshire Union line from Shrewsbury, via Wellington, to Stafford, had only been open three years when this unlikely collision took place on the morning of 29 July 1852. The locomotive involved was *Mazeppa*, a Crewe-built 2–2–2. It had arrived at Shrewsbury the previous evening, with a steam leak from the regulator. It could not be repaired while the locomotive was in steam, so the fire was dropped. Duly repaired by shed fitters, the fire was relit in the early morning. Of the two men on duty at the shed, one left on 'knocker-up' duties, then the other, after putting some more coal on *Mazeppa*'s fire, left for home ten minutes early at 5.50am. When the day cleaner arrived at 6.10am, ten minutes late, *Mazeppa* was not there. A platelayer had seen her steaming well along the line towards Wellington, with no one on the footplate.

The negligent fitter had left the locomotive in forward gear with the regulator open. As soon as there was sufficient boiler pressure, it had begun to move. The exhaust steam would have drawn on the fire and rapidly built up steam pressure. A locomotive standing in the yard, in steam, was sent out in hot pursuit, but it was too late. Fourteen miles from Shrewsbury, *Mazeppa* ran into the back of a Stafford-bound passenger train standing in Donnington station. Fortunately the short train was lightly loaded and the few passengers, one of whom was killed, were in the third-class coach nearest the engine.

into railways. However, the company's brief independence ended in 1847 when it agreed to a lease by the London and North Western Railway and within a couple of years the plan to turn the canals into railways had been dropped.

That was not the end of the Shropshire Union's interest in railways, however. Plans for a Shrewsbury to Stafford railway had been formulated before the 1846 Act, plans which, in conjunction with the Shrewsbury and Chester and Shrewsbury and Hereford companies, led to the provision of Shrewsbury's joint railway station. The Act of Parliament for the construction of the railway to Stafford was passed the same day as the SUR&CC Act – it would be one of very few railways to be built and operated in the UK by a canal company.

The Shropshire Union Railway from Shrewsbury to Stafford opened throughout on 1 June 1849.

The Fighting Shrewsburys

The 1840s saw a great deal of plotting and counter-plotting country-wide by the developing railway companies, over what they saw as 'their' territory and traffic. Many early railway schemes were rejected by Parliament as a result of objections by rivals. In Shropshire, there was a major battle between rival companies – a 'David and Goliath' battle whose weapons would primarily be business-related, spiced with one or two more physical acts. Though most of the drama occurred outside the county, the outcome defined the pattern of railway ownership in Shropshire and the routes that its trains would follow for many years.

In 1849, the Shrewsbury and Birmingham (S&B), and the Shrewsbury and Chester (S&C), were subject to hostile takeover bids by the London and North Western Railway (shades of the proposed Shropshire and Cheshire Railway). The LNWR now owned the main line through Wolverhampton to Crewe and beyond (the former Grand Junction) and the former Chester and Crewe Railway, which had been absorbed by the Grand Junction in 1840. It was constructing the Stour Valley line between Birmingham and Wolverhampton, but was not at all happy about a non-LNWR alternative route from Wolverhampton to Chester via Shrewsbury.

The S&C and the S&B had begun to cooperate even before the latter was completed and, once their lines were open, they began to cut fares to attract through traffic, breaking the LNWR's monopoly on traffic to Merseyside. The LNWR's general manager, Captain Mark Huish, began to threaten the Shrewsbury companies with the potential consequences of their actions. Even though the lines at either end of the route were under LNWR control, if not outright ownership, the Shrewsbury companies resisted, continuing their acts of defiance and suffering the consequences.

At Chester, the joint station committee refused to allow through bookings via the S&C/S&B beyond Wolverhampton. Objecting, the S&C's booking clerk was assaulted and thrown out.

At Wolverhampton, the LNWR deliberately delayed completion of the Stour Valley line. Through passengers from the S&B had to walk the mile to Wednesfield Heath station on the former Grand Junction. When in 1850 the S&B tried to trans-ship goods from the railway to the canal, a group of LNWR men tore up planking. In the scuffles that followed, one man's leg was broken, the local militia was called in and the Riot Act was read.

The Stour Valley line was completed by the end of 1850, but not opened. The LNWR could live without it, having the nearby Grand Junction line within its empire. In November 1851, the S&B tried to exercise its running powers by sending a train beyond Wolverhampton station – only to find the line blocked by an LNWR locomotive, behind which LNWR men were removing the rails.

Such tactics would hit the headlines, but the economic measures taken were at least as effective, if not more so. The direct route from Wolverhampton to Shrewsbury is very nearly 30 miles (48km); the LNWR implemented huge cuts in fares that made it much cheaper to travel via Stafford, more than 45 miles (72km), but entirely on LNWR-owned or -controlled metals. Similarly, the LNWR cut its freight rates to such an extent that goods began to flow along much longer LNWR routes, rather than follow the S&C and/or S&B. The LNWR could bear the inevitable losses; the Shrewsbury companies could not.

They needed to seek help – the GWR was busily constructing its own line to Wolverhampton and agreed to cooperate with the Shrewsbury companies. Freight began to move between the two, by canal connection until the GWR's lines were completed. Seeing the rapid approach of the inevitable outcome, the LNWR relented and allowed S&B trains to run up the Stour Valley line to Birmingham New Street from February 1854. In September of that year, the Shrewsbury companies amalgamated with the GWR and from 14 November trains from Shrewsbury ran through to Birmingham Snow Hill, on mixed-gauge tracks. A new section of railway from Stafford Road Junction diverted trains past the S&B's Stafford Road locomotive works and into the GWR's new Low Level station. In some part a measure of the importance of the route, Shrewsbury became, from 1855, the control centre for the GWR's northern division, encompassing the company's lines from Birmingham to Chester.

A matter of some significance to the GWR was the fact that the S&C and S&B had been built to standard gauge (4ft 8½in [1,435mm]). The GWR had originally been constructed to broad gauge (7ft ¼in [2,140mm]), but in 1846 Parliament's Gauge Commission had found in favour of standard gauge. Unlike some earlier acquisitions, the Wolverhampton–Shrewsbury–Chester railway was neither converted to broad gauge, nor operated (unlike the GWR southwards from Wolverhampton to Oxford) as a mixed-gauge railway. GWR broad gauge trains never ran in Shropshire.

The Shrewsbury and Hereford Railway

Shrewsbury was now connected to the growing national network, but it was not yet a significant railway centre. The 'hub' had only two spokes, with the junction at Wellington providing a third route. Two more major 'spokes' were needed to create a railway crossroads.

A line to the south formed one of these spokes from 21 April 1852, and Shrewsbury would henceforth be a true junction. The Shrewsbury and Hereford Railway opened on that day, though its trains at first ran only as far as Ludlow; its continuation to Hereford followed on 28 October 1853.

The S&H's Act of Parliament had been passed on 3 August 1846, the same day as the Shrewsbury and Birmingham and the Shropshire Union. Financial difficulties delayed the start of construction until 1850, when engineer Thomas Brassey (who had been the contractor for the Shrewsbury and Chester) agreed to handle the work for a 3.5 per cent shareholding. The formation – bridges, cuttings, embankments and so on – was constructed for a double-track railway, but only a single line

Miles	Stations
0	Shrewsbury
4¼	Condover
6¼	Dorrington
9½	Leebotwood
11¼	All Stretton Halt
12¾	Church Stretton
13¾	Little Stretton Halt
15¼	Marshbrook
18½	Wistanstow Halt
19¾	**Craven Arms** and Stokesay
22¾	Onibury
25	Bromfield
27¼	Ludlow
32	Woofferton
50¾ (82km)	*Hereford*

Closed
Outside county

was laid to keep costs down. Initially an independent company, the S&H was operated for its first ten years by Brassey. When his lease expired in 1862, it was taken up jointly by the LNWR, the GWR and the West Midland Railway.

Woofferton Junction station, near the county's southern border. In this view looking north, the line to Tenbury Wells runs to the right; 30 May 1953. J.E. NORRIS

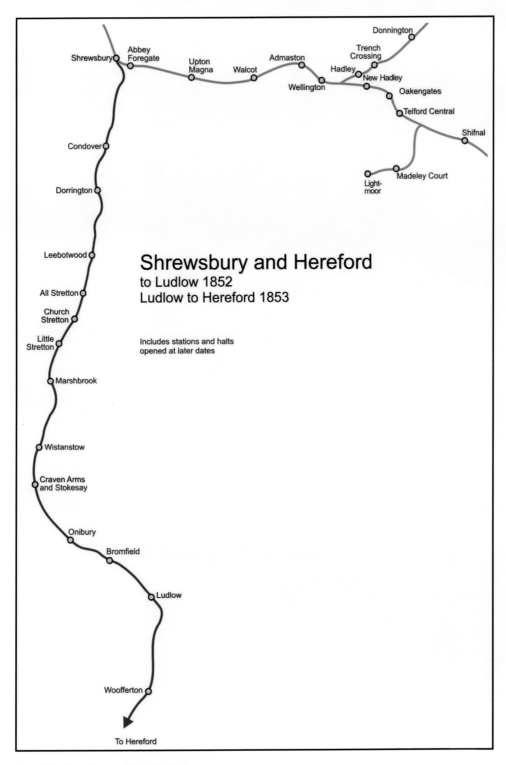

Map of the Shrewsbury and Hereford Railway.

That same year, the track was doubled – apart from Dinmore Tunnel in Herefordshire, which remained a single-bore bottleneck for a further thirty years, when a second bore was made, unusually on a different vertical alignment. On 1 August 1863, the West Midland Railway was absorbed by the Great Western. The Shrewsbury to Hereford railway was now effectively part of Shropshire's growing LNW/GW joint network and eight years later it was formally acquired by the GWR and LNWR.

The Crewe and Shrewsbury Railway

The Hereford line provided Shrewsbury with a link to South Wales, whose coalfield provided the GWR with its steam coal for most of its life. The high carbon content coal was also specified for use by the Royal Navy. During World War I, the 'Jellicoe Specials' carried great quantities of this fuel northwards, through Shropshire, on their way to Scapa Flow. But in 1852 the direct link northwards from

Shrewsbury did not exist – the coal would have had to travel via Chester or Stafford.

The Crewe line was Shropshire's first to be promoted by one of the major pre-grouping companies, the LNWR, receiving its Act of Parliament on 20 August 1853. Objections had been raised in the House of Lords regarding its intended route into Shrewsbury, but eventually running powers were arranged, enabling the line to enter Shrewsbury station. Like the Shrewsbury and Hereford, it opened as a single-line railway, with provision for a second set of rails, on 1 September 1858. Rapid development of a heavy traffic of coal northwards, and finished goods southwards, proved the viability of the route and the railway was doubled throughout from 1862.

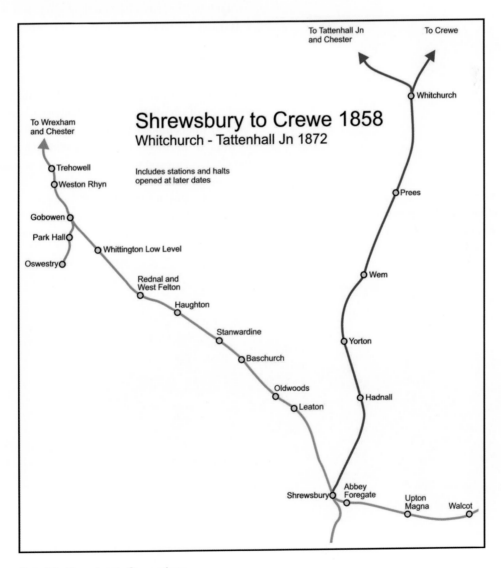

Map of the Shrewsbury to Crewe railway.

Miles	Stations
0	Shrewsbury
4¾	Hadnall
7	Yorton
10¾	Wem
14	Prees
18¾	Whitchurch
32½ (52km)	Crewe

Closed

Outside county

The LNWR line out of Shrewsbury: unique BR Pacific no. 71000 Duke of Gloucester *climbs away from the town with a 'North and West Express', on the stretch of railway appropriately known as 'Crewe Bank'.* RUSSELL MULFORD

Whitchurch to Chester

Whitchurch is only just within Shropshire. The Welsh border is about 2 miles (3km) west of the town centre and Cheshire is little over 1 mile (1.6km) to the north. The Shropshire town is noted for its Cheshire cheese and its name has appeared on railway stations far and wide, in the legend 'JOYCE WHITCHURCH' on the station clock. Established in 1690, the business, since 1964 part of Smith of Derby (after retirement of the last member of the Joyce family), continues in the town.

Whitchurch was also, for just over 100 years, a railway junction. Those years are spanned by the Cambrian connection (below), but for a time another line ran to the north and west, none of whose stations (other than Whitchurch) were within the county. Opened by the LNWR in 1872, the line to Tattenhall Junction, thence Chester, was seen by the company as providing a useful link in its route from Holyhead to South Wales. Bypassing the GWR's Shrewsbury and Chester, it was also a few miles shorter.

Despite the possibilities, it appears that the double-track line was not used significantly as a through route, except perhaps for diversions.

Whitchurch was no longer a junction when this photograph was taken in December 1971, but it still had extensive freight yards and the station was more or less intact. Today, the sidings have gone and the station is a shadow of its former self. SHROPSHIRE RAILWAY SOCIETY

OFF THE RAILS: SHREWSBURY, 1907

At 1.28am on 15 October, a heavy mail and sleeping car train approached Shrewsbury, its next stop. With portions from Glasgow, York and Liverpool, the train had been assembled at Crewe and would run down the 'North and West' to Hereford, Bristol and the west of England. It had left eight minutes late, but with ten-month-old 4–6–0 *Stephenson*, of the LNWR's Experiment Class at the head, the driver soon made up time, and was only three minutes late approaching Shrewsbury.

The Crewe line enters Shrewsbury station on a tight curve with a 10mph (16km/h) speed restriction, but when the train passed Crewe Bank signal box, just 600yd (550m) from the station, it was still travelling at full speed.

The locomotive derailed on the junction and overturned, with the train piling up behind it. The locomotive crew, two guards, three Post Office sorters and eleven passengers were killed.

The signals at Crewe Bank had been at danger; the train should by that point have been running much more slowly. Perhaps the driver had fallen asleep, or failed to appreciate where he was. On this fine clear night, the fireman should have realized things were not as they should be. It was the last of three (after Salisbury, 30 June 1906 and Grantham, 19 September 1906) excessive speed disasters in little over a year, all occurring at night, all unexplained.

Shrewsbury 1907: 4-6-0 Stephenson lies amid the wreckage of the night mail, after the inexplicable high-speed derailment at Crewe Junction. DAVE GIDDINS COLLECTION

Shrewsbury to Welshpool and the Minsterley Branch

Maps of Shropshire from the 1950s show seven lines radiating directly from the county town. One, the former 1866 'Potts' railway, belongs to the 'Minor Lines' chapter. Of the six remaining, four were in place from 1858 and remain so to this day. The other two were added in early 1862 – within days of each other. The Welshpool line remains open; the Severn Valley line survived as a through route for 101 years.

The railways to Welshpool and Minsterley were authorized by Act of Parliament in 1856. The main line ran from Coleham, in Shrewsbury, to Buttington, where it made a junction with the Oswestry and Newtown Railway (later to form part of the Cambrian Railways). Running powers enabled trains to reach Welshpool, a little less than 3 miles (5km) beyond Buttington. In common with many railways built at this time, it was proposed by an independent company, the Shrewsbury and Welshpool Railway, to be operated and maintained by an established company – in this case, the London and North Western Railway.

Because of difficulties with a tunnel near Middletown, just beyond the Welsh border, the branch line to Minsterley was completed before the main line, opening on 14 February 1861. Leaving

Miles	Stations
0	Shrewsbury
4¾	Hanwood*
7½	Yockleton
11	Westbury
13¼	Plas-y-Court Halt
17	*Buttington*
19¾ (32km)	Welshpool

*Hanwood is 4¾ miles from Shrewsbury in Shrewsbury–Welshpool timetables, and 5 miles in Minsterley branch timetables (LMS 1947 and BR(W) 1949)

Closed

Outside county

the main line at Cruckmeole Junction, near Hanwood, the branch would benefit from lead and other materials from the mines in the Stiperstones ore field. From 1877, Pontesbury would be connected to the richest mines by the narrow-gauge Snailbeach District Railways. Meanwhile, the tunnel near Middletown had become, in the hands of new contractors, a cutting, and the main line opened through to Buttington on 27 January 1862.

Like the Hereford and Crewe lines, it opened as a single-track railway. Unlike them, it was not

The end of the line at Minsterley – the wooden station buildings are still standing in 1971, twenty years after passenger services ended. SHROPSHIRE RAILWAY SOCIETY

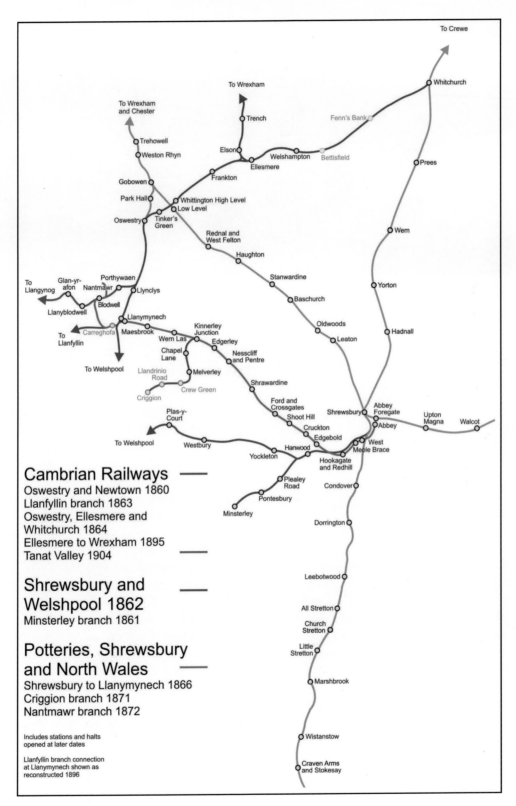

Map of the Cambrian Railways and the Shrewsbury and Welshpool Railway and their associated branches. It also shows the 'Potts' and the Tanat Valley Light Railway.

Cruckmeole Junction, where the Minsterley branch diverged from the Shrewsbury and Welshpool line. The Manors have gone and BR Standard Class 4 4-6-0 no. 75047 heads for Shrewsbury with the up Cambrian Coast Express on 30 April 1966. *BERWYN STEVENS*

Miles	Stations
0	Shrewsbury
5	Hanwood*
7	Plealey Road
8½	Pontesbury
10 (16km)	Minsterley

See note on page 32
Closed

doubled throughout – only the section to Cruck-meole Junction was so treated in 1866. The railway was run by the LNWR at first and from 1864 was leased by that company. During the same year, the GWR and LNWR Joint Committee was established; the following year, the line and its branch became part of the joint network.

Before the railways came to Britain, Welshpool was 'Pool' (the nearby Severn readily filling its flood plain after heavy rain). The prefix was added to avoid confusion with the Dorset town. A reminder of the original name lies 3 miles (5km) or so downstream, where Pool Quay was the highest navigable point on the Severn.

The Severn Valley

The present-day Severn Valley Railway (SVR) follows the river downstream, from its northern terminus at Bridgnorth to the Worcestershire riverside town of Bewdley. Here, it leaves the valley, swinging to the east and then north to its Kidderminster terminus, a superb recreation of a GWR station built from scratch by the preservationists. Not all passengers on the steam-hauled trains will realize that, between Bewdley and Kidderminster, they are not travelling on the original Severn Valley route. The original line continued down the valley to Stourport-on-Severn, before leaving the river to join the Birmingham–Kidderminster–Worcester line at Hartlebury Junction.

After some false starts (one of which would have taken the broad gauge into Shropshire), Shrewsbury's sixth spoke was provided for by an Act of 20 August 1853 (the same day as the Shrewsbury and Crewe), authorizing a line from the Oxford, Worcester and Wolverhampton Railway (OW&W) at Hartlebury to Shrewsbury. Further acts authorized some route alterations, before construction began in 1859 with the laying of a foundation stone

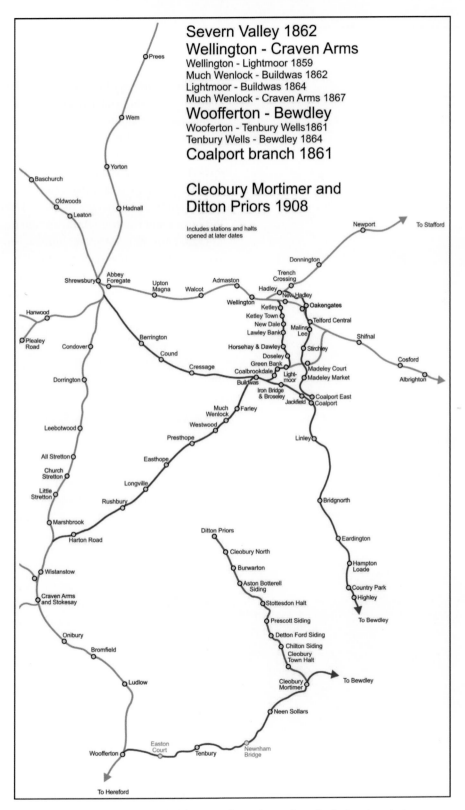

Map of the Severn Valley railway, the Wellington to Craven Arms railway, the Coalport branch, the Woofferton to Bewdley railway and the Cleobury Mortimer and Ditton Priors Light Railway.

Miles	Stations
0	Shrewsbury
4¼	Berrington
7¼	Cound Halt
8¼	Cressage
12¼	Buildwas
13¾	Iron Bridge and Broseley
15	Jackfield Halt
15¾	Coalport
18¼	Linley
22½	Bridgnorth
24¾	Eardington
27	Hampton Loade
29¼	Highley
35¼	*Bewdley*
52 (84km)	*Worcester Shrub Hill*

Closed
Severn Valley Railway
Outside county

at the site of the Victoria Bridge. The iron for this magnificent structure was cast at Coalbrookdale; the bridge itself lies entirely within Worcestershire, the county boundary being a mile or so upstream.

By the time that construction started, the Severn Valley Railway Company had reached agreement with the OW&W for the latter to run and maintain the line for its first five years. On 14 June 1860, an Act of Parliament enabled the OW&W to lease the SVR (for 999 years); two days later, a further Act authorized the merger of the OW&W with the Worcester and Hereford Railway, and the Newport, Abergavenny and Hereford Railway, to form the West Midlands Railway. It was the latter company that would operate the first train on the Severn Valley line from Worcester to Shrewsbury, on 1 February 1862.

In August 1863, the West Midlands Railway Company was taken over by the GWR and in July 1872 the Severn Valley Railway Company was absorbed by the GWR.

The Central Wales Line

From the junction at Craven Arms, a single-track railway meanders away into the south-western corner of Shropshire, home of Housman's 'quietest places under the sun'. Crossing the border just beyond the Welsh town of Knighton, trains run

Iron Bridge (two words) and Broseley station was very close to the 1779 bridge, as can be seen. Almost unknown when the line closed, Ironbridge (one word) is now a very popular destination for tourists and trippers – it is hard to imagine that the railway would not have been well patronized today. The photograph is undated, but appears to have been taken shortly after closure. IRONBRIDGE GORGE MUSEUM TRUST

through mid-Wales spa country to arrive eventually at Swansea.

The railway's existence stems from expansionary plans by the London and North Western Railway. Although LNWR was able to run trains to Hereford on the joint line from Shrewsbury, a connection into the valuable South Wales coal market was desirable. Nevertheless, the route was not built directly by the LNWR, but by local companies supported by the LNWR.

Starting at Craven Arms, the Knighton Railway, wholly in Shropshire, was opened for goods in 1860 and passengers in 1861. Within four years, the Central Wales Railway, projected as an extension of the Knighton Railway, had opened to Llandrindod Wells. Three years later, in 1868, the Central Wales Extension Railway took the line to Llandovery; the three companies were absorbed into the LNWR the same year. The LNWR then had to use running powers to get to Pontardulais, from where its own

Map of the Craven Arms to Knighton railway (Central Wales line) and the Bishop's Castle Railway.

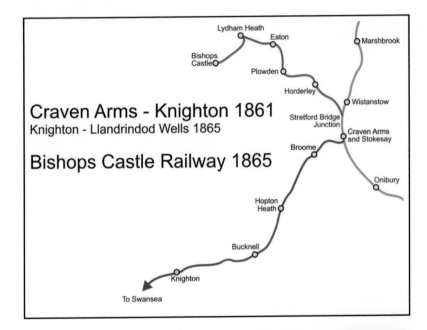

Craven Arms - Knighton 1861
Knighton - Llandrindod Wells 1865

Bishops Castle Railway 1865

BELOW: LNWR 4-6-2T no. 2667 stands at Knighton station with an express train on the Central Wales line in the pre-grouping era.
G.M. PERKINS/KIDDERMINSTER RAILWAY MUSEUM

Miles	Stations
0	Craven Arms
3½	Broome
5	Hopton Heath
8	Bucknell
12¼	Knighton
95½ (154km)	*Swansea (Victoria)*

Closed
Outside county

metals led to Swansea Victoria. It had gained access to the coalfield and a passenger service to south-west Wales's major port, some 115 miles (185km) from Shrewsbury and 95 miles (153km) from the junction at Craven Arms.

The line from Craven Arms to Knighton was originally single track. Doubled from 1871, it was reduced to single track again when the line was rationalized in the 1960s.

Madeley Junction to Lightmoor

The Shrewsbury and Birmingham Railway (S&B) had completed its main line from the county town to Wolverhampton in 1849; a branch towards

Coalbrookdale would tap into potentially valuable traffic. That branch was authorized in July 1847, completed as far as Lightmoor in 1854 and fully opened the following year. It joined the main line at Madeley Junction, so-named after the town some 3 miles (5km) to the south, served by an intermediate station. At Lightmoor, it connected with the Coalbrookdale network of mineral tramways.

The original plans for the line had included a triangular junction with the main line, but only the east-to-south connection was constructed. Similarly, the line had been authorized to descend from Lightmoor into Coalbrookdale, but funds were insufficient for the S&B to carry this forward at the time. Other matters were coming to fruition – the S&B amalgamated with the GWR shortly after the branch was completed and other plans were being developed for railways in the area. Ultimately, the branch would form a link into the Wellington–Buildwas–Much Wenlock line that would pass through Lightmoor.

Of the routes that eventually converged at Buildwas, it was the first to lose its passenger service, but would eventually become the last link to the main-line network, carrying fuel trains to Ironbridge Power Station. Lightmoor station was actually closed when the line from Lightmoor to Buildwas opened in 1864, though a basic 'Lightmoor Platform' was opened a little nearer Coalbrookdale in 1907. Madeley station was renamed 'Madeley Court' (after the nearby sixteenth-century manor house) in 1884,

6849 Walton Grange *heads for Wolverhampton with the 5.20pm all stations to Wolverhampton on 14 July 1965. Its days are numbered – as are those of Madeley Junction signal box, which was replaced by a modern BR structure, between the main line and the branch, in 1969.* BERWYN STEVENS

then renamed 'Madeley (Salop)' in 1897. Passenger services on the branch were withdrawn in March 1915 as a war economy measure, reinstated in July 1925, then withdrawn permanently just two months later. General goods traffic continued until 1963; Kemberton Colliery, which had opened in 1864, continued to be served until it closed in 1967. Ironbridge Power Station is due to close in 2015; the Telford Steam Railway has designs on the line from Lightmoor to Coalbrookdale and Buildwas, but it seems unlikely that the Madeley Junction to Lightmoor line has a future beyond that date.

Dark Lane branch

Largely forgotten today, a short mineral line was constructed by the GWR to serve industry – iron works and a brick works – in the Stirchley and Randlay area. It left the main Shrewsbury to Wolverhampton line by a west-facing junction at the south-eastern end of Hollinswood yard, which connected to the Lilleshall Company's steel works and railway system to the north. Just 1¼ miles (2km) long, it opened in 1908 and closed with the yard early in 1959. The site of the junction now lies beneath the huge and busy Hollinswood Interchange (through which the main line passes), more or less at the south end of today's Telford Central station.

Wellington to Craven Arms

This railway opened in no fewer than five sections. On 30 May 2012, the Olympic Torch was carried through the small Shropshire town of Much Wenlock and the curious cyclopean mascot of the London Olympics bore the name 'Wenlock' for the same reason. It was here in 1850 that Dr William Penny Brookes held his first 'Olympian Games', on the town's racecourse. Those games led to the development of the Olympic movement nationally and are acknowledged to have been one of the forces behind the modern games.

Wenlock's racecourse is long gone and the town may feel like a backwater today, but it has a long history. Its monastery was founded in AD680 and it

Miles	Stations
0	Wellington
1½	Ketley
2	Ketley Town Halt
2½	New Dale Halt
3	Lawley Bank
4	Horsehay and Dawley
4¾	Doseley Halt
5½	Lightmoor Platform
6¼	Green Bank Halt
7	Coalbrookdale
8	Buildwas
10¼	Farley Halt
11¼	Much Wenlock
13	Westwood Halt
14¼	Presthope
16¼	Easthope Halt
18	Longville
20¼	Rushbury
22¾	Harton Road
27	Wistanstow Halt
28½ (46km)	Craven Arms

Closed
Telford Steam Railway

was granted borough status by Edward IV in 1468 – a status that lasted for very nearly 500 years. The development of Telford (Dawley, in its first incarnation) encompassed large parts of the borough, including Coalbrookdale and Madeley, and it was abolished in 1966. Around 100 years earlier, however, Wenlock was clearly a town of some significance and thus required a railway. Among other things, people would need to be able to get to the Olympian Games …

The signal box is 'Horsehay', but the station is 'Horsehay and Dawley'. It closed with the railway from Wellington to Much Wenlock and the buildings have since been demolished, but the platform remains to this day, served by the trains of the Telford Steam Railway. RUSSELL MULFORD

Wellington–Lightmoor: The Wellington and Severn Junction Railway commenced at Ketley Junction, about 1¼ miles (2km) east of Wellington station on the Wolverhampton line. It opened for freight to Horsehay in 1857 and to Lightmoor, where it joined the line from Madeley Junction, the following year. The junction faced Coalbrookdale; when a passenger service commenced on 2 May 1859, trains ran from Wellington to Lightmoor, then reversed to continue via Madeley to Shifnal (and vice versa).

Much Wenlock–Buildwas: Shortly after the above service began, the Wenlock and Severn Junction's Act received its Royal Assent. It opened the same day as the Severn Valley, on 1 February 1862. Its ruling gradient of 1 in 40 was a fearsome climb in steam days.

Buildwas–Coalbrookdale and Lightmoor–Coalbrookdale: Two different companies were involved in the construction of this continuous stretch of railway.

In July 1861, the Much Wenlock, Craven Arms and Coalbrookdale Extension Railway obtained its Act and would henceforth be the 'Wenlock Railway Company'. The GWR would help with the construction of the line to Coalbrookdale – no great distance, but the crossing of the Severn required a very substantial bridge. The Albert Edward Bridge is remarkably similar to its counterpart, the Victoria Bridge, further down the Severn Valley line near Arley. Like the Victoria Bridge, its major iron components were 'Cast and erected by the Coalbrookdale Company'. Unlike the Victoria Bridge, it carried a double-track railway.

A few days after the Wenlock Act, the GWR received authorization for its own extension, the long-awaited line from Lightmoor to Coalbrookdale. The viaduct that curves across the head of the dale on a steep gradient is almost immediately above the 'coke hearth', the site of Darby's successful experiments in modern iron-making. Opening from Lightmoor to Buildwas on 1 November 1864, the works that gave the world its first iron rails was at last connected to the modern railway.

Much Wenlock–Craven Arms: Construction was already well under way when the Coalbrookdale line opened. Just over a month later, on 5 December 1864, the line southwards opened to goods traffic for the 3 miles (5km) to Presthope. Limestone quarries in the vicinity now had their rail connection and the impetus for the remainder of the extension may then have been lost. It would be another three years before the last 11 miles (18km) of railway were completed, again with assistance from the GWR. Beyond Presthope, the line cut through the Wenlock Edge in a short tunnel, to descend gradually into Ape Dale on the western side, joining the Hereford line at Marsh Farm Junction. On 16 December 1867, passenger trains began to run between Wellington and Craven Arms.

Coalbrookdale station, as seen in the years before World War I. Coalbrookdale church and the Ironbridge Institute are prominent in the background. IRONBRIDGE GORGE MUSEUM TRUST

The Cambrian Railways: Whitchurch to Welshpool

The Cambrian Railways Company (always plural) owned, at the grouping, some 230 route miles (370km). Stretching from Brecon in the south to Pwllheli in the north-west, its main line ran between Shropshire's Whitchurch and Aberystwyth. Its numerous branch lines included the Wrexham branch from Ellesmere and the Llanfyllin branch from Llanymynech. None of its lines within Shropshire remain within the national network.

The plurality of the company's name reflects its formation, the main line being formed of the metals of no fewer than five companies. In route order, these were: the Oswestry, Ellesmere and Whitchurch; the Oswestry and Newtown; the Llanidloes and Newtown; the Newtown and

Nearly twenty years after the last freight, Longville station, on the Much Wenlock to Craven Arms line, was reasonably intact when photographed in February 1983.

Machynlleth; and the Aberystwith (*sic*) and Welch (*sic*) Coast railways. An Act of 25 July 1864 amalgamated the first four of those companies to form the Cambrian Railways Company; the Aberystwyth company followed in 1865. Within Shropshire, the Oswestry and Newtown opened on 1 May 1860, with its Porthywaen mineral branch opening the same year. The Oswestry, Ellesmere and Whitchurch opened two days after the Cambrian Railways Company was formed, on 27 July 1864.

In 1865, the Cambrian Railways Company settled into Oswestry (in Shropshire), with its head office in the magnificent station buildings and the substantial locomotive works nearby. Its population doubling over the following forty years, Oswestry became a railway town, though it was perhaps more an Inverurie than a Crewe.

Miles	Stations
0	Whitchurch
3	Fenn's Bank
6¾	Bettisfield
7¾	Welshampton
10¾	Ellesmere
12¾	Frankton
16¼	Whittington High Level
17¼	Tinker's Green Halt
18¼	Oswestry
22	Llynclys
23¼	Pant (Salop)
24¼	Llanymynech
33¼	Welshpool
47¾	Newtown
95¾ (154km)	Aberystwyth

Closed
Cambrian Heritage Railways
Outside county

Oswestry is very much a border town, Wales being just over 3 miles (5km) from Oswestry station. To reach Whitchurch on the Shrewsbury–Crewe line, the tracks crossed into Wales between Bettisfield and Fenn's Bank; 6 miles (10km) south of Oswestry, the Cambrian entered Wales – and remained there.

Llanfyllin Branch

Only the first few hundred yards of the line to Llanfyllin lay in Shropshire – though they constituted an interesting few hundred yards. Llanfyllin lies in the Cain Valley (there is a River Abel too, which joins the Cain at Llanfyllin) and its limestone quarries attracted the early railway builders. The Oswestry and Newtown Railway's branch line ran from Llanymynech and opened for traffic in 1863.

The interest in the first few hundred yards derives from its curious junction arrangement. To avoid the cost of crossing the Ellesmere to Newtown Canal, just to the west of Llanymynech, the branch was constructed to be accessed by the 'rock siding', which crossed over the canal north of the station. Trains would leave Llanymynech in a northerly direction and then reverse along the siding and onwards to Llanfyllin.

A few years later, the ill-fated Potteries, Shrewsbury and North Wales Company had no qualms about costs. It built its railway through Llanymynech to the Nantmawr quarries to cross under the Oswestry and Newtown Railway, the canal and the Llanfyllin branch. After the 'Potts' closed in 1880, the Cambrian took on the line to Nantmawr and, in 1894, set about connecting the Llanfyllin branch to the Nantmawr branch of the 'Potts' at Wern Junction and reconstructed (by agreement with the receiver) the crossing of the railways at Llanymynech on the level. From 1896, trains for Llanfyllin could leave Llanymynech in a southerly direction, without reversal.

Ellesmere to Wrexham

The Cambrian Railways had close associations with the London and North Western Railway, which had sponsored the Oswestry to Whitchurch

On 28 August 1926, just three years after the grouping, former Cambrian Railways 4-4-0 no. 19 stands beneath the signal gantry at Oswestry station. As GWR no. 1089, it is starting to show signs of new ownership. H.C. CASSERLEY

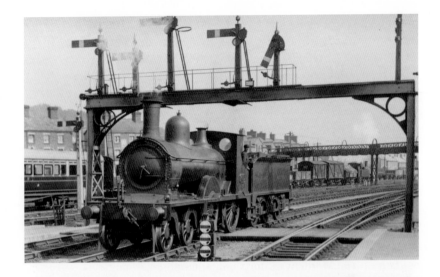

After years of neglect, the station building at Oswestry once again reflects the town's former importance as HQ of the Cambrian Railways Company. Seen in February 2013, a signal has recently been re-erected (extreme right) by the preservationists.

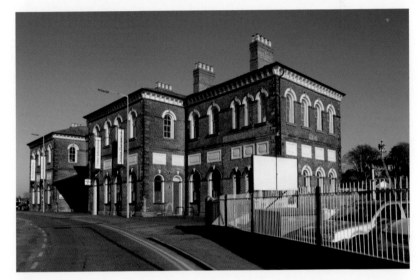

OFF THE RAILS: WELSHAMPTON, 1897

On 11 June 1897, a Sunday school excursion ran from Royton, Lancashire, to Barmouth, travelling over the Cambrian main line through Shropshire. Hauled by two Cambrian 0–6–0 goods engines, it consisted of fifteen coaches – fourteen Cambrian vehicles (a mixture of bogie and six-wheeled stock) and a four-wheeled Lancashire and Yorkshire Railway (L&YR) brake van. This vehicle was at the front of the train on its return journey. Passing through Welshampton, virtually the whole train – the tender of the second locomotive and all the coaches apart from the last two – became derailed. The inspecting officer, Lieut. Col. H.A. Yorke, described the train as 'totally wrecked'. Nine people were killed and two others died within days as a result.

Earlier in the day, a Cambrian guard had complained of the rough riding of the (L&YR) van and the company insisted that this was the cause, but Yorke, in his report, blamed poorly maintained and inadequate track, with light rails and rotten sleepers. Excessive speed (perhaps 45mph [72km/h]) was the secondary cause. The track had spread beneath the oscillating second tender, causing it to fall between the rails, and the rest of the train inevitably followed. The Cambrian Railways Company was at the time engaged in relaying its network with heavier rails – unfortunately, it had not at that time dealt with Welshampton.

line, and the Wrexham, Mold and Connah's Quay Railway (WM&CQ). Making an end-on connection with the latter at Wrexham Central, the Ellesmere to Wrexham line was built jointly by the WM&CQ and the Cambrian, but operated entirely by the latter. It opened on 2 November 1895.

The line was conceived in the Welsh Railways Through Traffic Act of 1889. The legislation was passed as part of an attempt to divert traffic away from the North and West route via Hereford. Its central main line would be formed of the Cambrian from Oswestry to Llanidloes, thence the Mid-Wales Railway via Three Cocks Junction to Talyllyn Junction and onwards to South Wales by the Brecon and Merthyr, or the Neath and Brecon. Oswestry would link to the GWR and the LNWR and via the Wrexham and Ellesmere, to North Wales.

In the event, the Wrexham and Ellesmere never saw substantial long-distance traffic. The longer Through Traffic Act route was heavily used during World War I by the 'Jellicoe' coal specials running from the South Wales coalfield to the north of Scotland – but they travelled via Ellesmere to Whitchurch, not Wrexham. The Mid-Wales Railway, suffering from financial problems, became part of the Cambrian formally in 1904.

Miles	Stations
0	Ellesmere
1¼	Elson Halt
2¾	Trench Halt
12¾ (21km)	Wrexham (Central)*

*Wrexham Central station was relocated 250m further west in 1998
Closed
Outside county

The Coalport Branch

The remnants of three different transport systems can be seen at the Blists Hill Victorian Town Museum, near Madeley. The road approach from the north, Legges Way, was constructed partly on the trackbed of the Coalport branch. Perhaps 200yd (180m) beyond the museum entrance, a skeletal iron bridge high above the road once bore the plateway taking coal from the Meadow Pit to the canal. That canal is still in water through the museum site.

The Shropshire Canal had opened for traffic in 1791. Connected to the growing canal network at Donnington Wood, it ran southwards to Coalport,

Whitchurch, at the Cambrian's north-eastern extremity, 1952: 'Dukedog' 9020 will have arrived with a train from the Cambrian line and, having just turned, will undoubtedly depart along the same metals.
RUSSELL MULFORD

with a branch towards the head of Coalbrookdale. It was fairly intensively worked, mostly short-haul traffic, but some freight was trans-shipped onto the Severn at Coalport.

The London and North Western Railway leased the canal from 1849, but soon realized that it was in need of repair, suffering from subsidence and loss of water. An 1857 Act of Parliament granted the LNWR the right to purchase the canal and to convert it into a railway. The area served by the western branch of the canal was by now rail-connected – only Coalport needed a railway. Opening for freight in 1860, the passenger service began on 10 August 1861; the station at Malins Lee opened a year later, on 7 July 1862.

The branch commenced at Hadley Junction, on the Wellington to Stafford line – the Shropshire Union. It climbed through Oakengates to Priors Lee siding, ran south through Malins Lee and Dawley and Stirchley stations, and then began the fearful descent to Coalport. Starting at 1 in 50 to Madeley Market, after a short 1 in 65 it steepened to 1 in 31 for about a quarter of a mile (400m), followed by a mile (1,600m) at 1 in 40 to the limits of Coalport station. A cautious descent to the terminus was needed; there would have been fireworks ascending the 1 in 31 stretch.

Plans for further expansion and extension had been prepared as early as 1857. By means of a river

Miles	Stations
0	Wellington
1½	Hadley
3¼	Oakengates
4¾	Malins Lee
6	Dawley & Stirchley
7½	Madeley Market
9½ (15km)	Coalport North

Closed

crossing beyond Coalport station and a junction with the Severn Valley line, the branch could have been part of a through route to Worcester. Nothing came of those plans.

Wellington to Nantwich and Market Drayton to Stoke

About half a mile (800m) west of Wellington, the site of the former Drayton Junction is now difficult to spot. The GWR line via Market Drayton to Nantwich in Cheshire gave the company access, through running powers, to Crewe. Like so many relative latecomers to the railway map, it survived barely 100 years.

Coalport: normal passenger services had ended three years before this rail tour visited the terminus on 23 April 1955. Earlier in the day, the train had travelled along the freight-only remnant of the Craven Arms line from Much Wenlock to Longville; later, it would run on the Minsterley branch, which was also freight-only by this time. The locomotive was GWR 'Dean Goods' Class no. 2516, one of the last survivors of the class, now preserved in the museum at Swindon. RUSSELL MULFORD

The line was not conceived as a through route. The northern part of the line, the 10 miles (16km) from Nantwich's Market Drayton Junction to the town of that name, was opened by the Nantwich and Market Drayton Railway in 1863. Initially, it had been intended that the LNWR would work the line, but in the event it was operated by the GWR, remaining independent until taken over by the GWR in 1897.

The southern leg, the 16 miles (26km) from Wellington to Market Drayton, was opened four years later as the Wellington and Drayton Railway. The company was incorporated in 1862, with support from the GWR, and initial plans envisaged the railway continuing beyond Market Drayton to various points to the north and east. However, alliance with the Nantwich and Market Drayton, and running powers beyond as far as Manchester, meant that no further construction was required.

An Act of 1864 authorized absorption by the GWR on completion of the line, which was formalized

Miles	Stations
0	Wellington
2¾	Longdon Halt
4¾	Crudgington
7	Rowton Halt
7¼	Ellerdine Halt
8¾	Peplow
11	Hodnet
12	Wollerton Halt
13¾	Tern Hill
16¾	Market Drayton
20¼	Adderley
27½	*Nantwich*
32 (51km)	*Crewe*

Closed
Outside county

5955 Garth Hall *has halted its southbound freight to take water at Market Drayton on 15 July 1965. Virtually nothing remains today of the former junction station.* BERWYN STEVENS

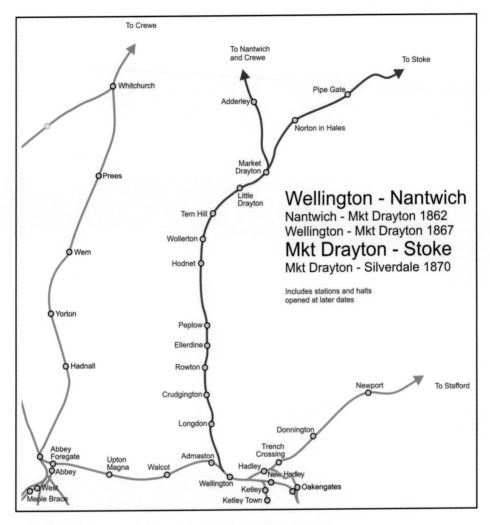

Map of the Wellington to Nantwich railway and the North Staffs line from Stoke.

in 1877. Meanwhile, the Nantwich and Market Drayton Railway had doubled its track, so that from 1867 the GWR had an effective route through to Crewe and Manchester.

Market Drayton was, of course, the main station en route. Stations and associated facilities were also provided at Crudgington, Peplow, Hodnet and Tern Hill, all south of Drayton, and at Adderley and, in Cheshire, Audlem.

Other than the minor lines, the railways of Shropshire were almost all in the hands of the GWR

or the LNWR, later LMS – but there were two exceptions. The Cambrian was of some significance. The 6-mile (10km) incursion of the North Staffordshire Railway from Stoke and Newcastle-under-Lyme to Market Drayton was not a major part of the railway network. However, by extending westwards from Silverdale, the North Staffs effectively thwarted any remaining expansion plans that the GWR might have had. Opened in February 1870, the first two stations from Market Drayton, at Norton-in-Hales and Pipe Gate, were in Shropshire.

SHROPSHIRE RAILWAYMEN – 'PICCOLO PETE' JOHNSON

The late 'Piccolo Pete' Johnson's very readable accounts of his experiences on the footplate were published in 1980 by Bradford Barton as *Through the Links at Crewe*. Most of his career on the railways was spent there with the London Midland region, but he actually began work as a cleaner with the GWR at Wellington in 1944, towards the end of World War II. Born in Birmingham, he had been evacuated to live with his uncle in Ironbridge.

Promotion to fireman in October that year took Pete to Gresty Lane, the GWR shed at Crewe, from where he regularly worked the Market Drayton line. He tells of struggles with an ancient Aberdare Class locomotive, an outside-framed, inside-cylindered 2–6–0 that had a hit-and-miss reverser and was steaming badly, and a drenching on an ex-LNWR 0–8–0 ('the most uncomfortable engines I ever had to work on'). Borrowed to haul a Gresty Lane to Hollinswood freight, such arrangements, made from time to time, required the loco to return straight away, light, unless there was a load that could be worked back immediately. There was no such load at Hollinswood, so it was back to Crewe. They could have run to Oxley and turned, but it was a warm summer afternoon, so, to save time, they set off, tender first. The warm summer afternoon ended with a thunderstorm

and torrential rain. With no shelter possible, Pete and the driver were thoroughly drenched.

Perhaps the most memorable incident involved another light engine trip along the Market Drayton line. It was not uncommon for enginemen to (unofficially) drop a little loco coal for their colleagues' stoves and on this occasion there was one particularly large lump in the tender of the 43XX 2–6–0 being taken from Oxley to Crewe one night. Rather than break it up for the firebox, they would 'save it for Ronnie at Crudgington'. Pete explains how he expected they would stop to drop it into his coal bunker, but in fact they drove through at around 40mph (64km/h), nudging the lump out of the cab at the appropriate spot. This may not have been wise. The coal smashed through the bunker and continued through the ground floor of the signal box, wrecking the signalman's steps en route before wreaking havoc with the wires and point rodding and ending up on the station platform. Immediately the wires were hit, the signals all went to danger and Pete and his driver had to stop – to return to the station and discover the effects of their delivery. As far as the subsequent internal enquiry was concerned, the coal had merely fallen off the tender; reading between Pete's lines, one suspects a little devilment in the evening's escapade …

Scene of Piccolo Pete's 'coal drop', Crudgington station is seen after closure of the line, in 1970. The last passenger train had called in 1963; the last freight passed in 1967. SHROPSHIRE RAILWAY SOCIETY

Miles	Stations
0	Market Drayton
3¼	Norton-in-Hales
5¾	Pipe Gate, for Woore
16¾ (27km)	*Stoke-on-Trent*

Closed
Outside county

Miles	Stations
0	Woofferton
2¾	*Easton Court*
5¼	Tenbury Wells
8½	*Newnham Bridge*
10¾	Neen Sollars
14¼	Cleobury Mortimer
16¼	Wyre Forest
20¾	*Bewdley*
24¼ (39km)	*Kidderminster*

Closed
Severn Valley Railway
Outside county

Woofferton to Bewdley

The line from Woofferton to Bewdley threaded the southern boundaries of Shropshire. After leaving Shropshire's Woofferton Junction, on the Hereford line, trains would pass into Herefordshire to stop at Easton Court and then return to Shropshire for Tenbury Wells. The Worcestershire town was south of the Teme, but its the station was in Burford, Shropshire. Newnham Bridge station, the next stop, was in Worcestershire. Trains then left the Teme Valley and climbed back into Shropshire to call at Neen Sollars and, after another brief incursion into Worcestershire, Cleobury Mortimer. In 1908, the latter became the junction for the Cleobury Mortimer and Ditton Priors Light Railway.

The last stop was at Wyre Forest station, in Worcestershire. Deep within the ancient forest, the Dowles Brook forms the county boundary and the railway remained on the southern side before leaving the forest, crossing the river to join the Severn Valley line at Dowles Junction. The latter was not a true junction – the mile of double-track railway to Bewdley was operated as two single-track lines running beside each other.

The route from Woofferton to Newnham Bridge had been used some years previously by the rather unsuccessful Leominster Canal. Intended to link Leominster with the Severn near Stourport, the eastern section was never completed. A tunnel east of Marlbrook was completed, but collapsed, and there were insufficient funds to finish the work. The western section operated for sixty years, but the company was never able to pay a dividend. In 1858, the canal was bought by the Shrewsbury and Hereford Railway Company, which drained the canal to sell off the land – part of which was used by the railway.

The railway was built and opened in two sections, by two different companies. The Tenbury Railway Company built the line from Woofferton, gaining its Act of Parliament the same year as the canal closed, in 1859. It opened to traffic just two years later, on 1 August 1861. Within a year, the Shrewsbury and Hereford was the property of the GWR (and the West Midland Railway) and the LNWR; the Tenbury Railway, although worked by the GWR, also became part of the GWR/LNWR joint network.

The remainder was pure GWR. Promoted by the Tenbury and Bewdley Railway Company, incorporated in 1860, the line took four years to build and opened in 1864. It was worked from the outset by the GWR and absorbed by that company five years later.

49

The GWR's railcars were seen on the Severn Valley line and, as in this photograph taken at Cleobury Mortimer, on the Bewdley to Woofferton Junction line; 15 July 1961. ARCHIVE IMAGES

Shrewsbury Station

Construction of Shrewsbury station was funded by the four companies whose lines were the first to serve the town: the Shrewsbury and Chester; Shrewsbury and Birmingham; Shrewsbury and Hereford; and the Shropshire Union Railways. The first trains on the Shrewsbury and Chester had arrived at a temporary terminus; use of the new station began when the joint line from the east opened in June 1849. At first, two main through platforms were provided, but within ten years there were five platforms, covered by an overall roof 450ft (140m) long, with a span of 70ft (20m). Like many such stations in early times, small turntables served short stretches of track, cutting across the running lines and platforms. Horses were used to shunt the four-wheeled carriages used in those early times, enabling relatively easy swapping of 'through carriages' between trains. Hard to imagine today, the practice inevitably died out when longer coaches came into service.

Low winter sunshine highlights the ironwork of Shrewsbury station's extension over the Severn, built in the early years of the twentieth century. Behind can be seen the arches of the original bridge.

Shrewsbury station's massive overall roof, at the southern end of the station, dated from the early years of the twentieth century. Its removal was completed in 1963, just a couple of years after 45145 was recorded on one of the through roads on the east side of the station. Left, behind the signal, a wagon stands on the link to the Shropshire Union yard. RUSSELL MULFORD

It was perhaps also inevitable that, as further routes developed and traffic grew, the original layout would become inadequate. At the turn of the twentieth century, a major expansion took place. Perhaps the best-known part of this expansion affected the main station building and its forecourt. It was extended to the left, to Castle Foregate – and, unusually, downwards. The original forecourt met the main entrance at platform level. It was excavated to serve the new main entrance, created directly beneath the original. On the face of it, this was an astonishing achievement. It was certainly a major undertaking, though it should be remembered that there were already extensive cellars and deep foundations. In the early days, passengers had accessed the far platforms using the Dana Footbridge (the bridge took the place of a pre-existing path to some open ground, named after the Rev. Dana, beside the gaol). The new lower-level entrance feeds directly into today's subway.

Once within the station, passengers would see more substantial changes. The lines immediately south of the original station crossed the Severn on a seven-arch bridge carrying three lines of rails. The extension involved building two new steel spans, supported on cast-iron columns in the middle of the river, on each side of the original bridge. The platforms were then extended over the river – the original main platform with two new bays and one greatly enlarged island, also with two new bays. The main platform now measured a little over 400yd (370m), the island being slightly shorter. There were now nine tracks across the river: the platform roads; a through road beyond the outer face of the island; and another leading to a dock platform and the Shropshire Union yard. Other than these two tracks, the whole southern part of the station, from the Dana Footbridge to the limits of the extended platforms, was then covered by a huge overall glazed steel roof, with a footbridge spanning the tracks at the southern end. The smaller overall roof at the north end of the station was removed in 1924 and replaced with canopies. This station layout would serve the town until the 1960s.

Abbey Curve

Between the Hereford and Wolverhampton lines, immediately south of Shrewsbury station, is the Abbey Curve. This double-track link was opened on 1 May 1867, enabling traffic between those lines to pass through Shrewsbury without having to enter the station and reverse. In addition to freight traffic, it was used for many years by the direct

Two Shrewsbury ticket collectors pose for the photographer in their GWR and LNWR Joint uniforms. RUSSELL MULFORD COLLECTION

passenger trains running from London and the West Midlands to the Welsh coast. It remains in regular use for freight to the present day.

Bradshaw – Passenger Train Services at the End of an Era

1922 is a useful date for a retrospective look at train services in Shropshire. The last year before the 1923 grouping, the zenith for Britain's railways was, if it had not already passed, only a little way ahead. Although great things were still to come in the days of the 'Big Four', changes were apparent. Most of the country's railways had been built, with just a handful of lines still to come. The great depression had not yet happened, but the railways' stronghold on freight traffic was already being eaten into by war surplus road vehicles, driven by survivors of that war. In terms of lines offering a passenger service, Shropshire's peak had already passed. The years from 1911 to 1915 saw services on all the lines that ever carried a passenger service – in 1915, the lightly used Lightmoor to Shifnal service ended. Three of the county's minor lines lost their passenger services in the 1930s, but there would be no more passenger closures before nationalization. Some of Shropshire's railway passenger facilities had not yet materialized – numerous halts would be opened by the GWR in the 1930s.

Bradshaw's Guide for July 1922 paints, somewhat indirectly, a fascinating picture of passenger

The LNWR side of Shrewsbury shed in the years before the grouping. Lady of the Lake Class 2-2-2 no. 44 stands beside a 'Renown' Class 4-cylinder compound 4-4-0. LENS OF SUTTON

services in Shropshire. That picture is, in parts, astonishingly complex. The main lines carried a very wide range of services, with through trains and/or through carriages serving destinations far and wide. Some main-line trains might well arrive at their final destinations with the same set of coaches that they started with, possibly even the same locomotive. Others would divide part way along their route, and/or would stop to attach coaches. Pity the poor traveller in the wrong portion of a train! There are some (very) early morning trains in the main-line timetables, their prime purpose being to convey the Royal Mail and news-papers, which were invariably carried by rail for most of their journeys.

Main Lines: Wolverhampton to Chester

This was Shropshire's main line, the Great Western route to Merseyside, albeit Birkenhead rather than Liverpool. Bradshaw details, on pages 84 to 89 'London, Birmingham, Wolverhampton, Shrewsbury, Oswestry and Chester', services between Birmingham Snow Hill and Chester and indicates through and connecting trains to and from Paddington and Birkenhead. We will consider northbound trains; a balancing pattern of services ran in the opposite direction.

The first through train northbound left Paddington fifteen minutes after midnight, arrived in Shrewsbury at 5.22am, left again eleven minutes later to arrive at Chester at 6.45am and finally Birkenhead at 7.47am. The 9.10am from Paddington was a 'Birmingham and North Express', with a 'Breakfast and Luncheon Car' and a through carriage to Pwllheli, running via the GWR Ruabon–Dolgellau line. The 10.40am from Paddington, another 'Birmingham and North Express', con-veyed a Luncheon Car and through carriages from Paddington to Aberystwyth and Towyn (via Welshpool), and from Birmingham Snow Hill to Barmouth and Pwllheli. The last through train, another 'Birmingham and North Express', was the 6.10pm, due to arrive in Birkenhead exactly five hours later. Including a dining car, 'Paddington to Wolverhampton', its schedule of just three hours and ten minutes made it the fastest train to Shrewsbury.

Not all northbound trains originated at Paddington. The 'Aberystwyth Express' left Birmingham Snow Hill at 9.10am and, after calling at Wolverhampton Low Level, passed through the county non-stop, via Shrewsbury's Abbey Curve to Welshpool. There it combined with a Birkenhead (via Whitchurch and Oswestry) to Aberystwyth service, delivering passengers to the Welsh resort and university town at 1.40pm.

Other long-distance trains ran along at least part of the main line including a number travelling to Manchester (London Road). One such, originating from Bournemouth, would split at Wolverhampton. The Manchester portion would call at Wellington and then run non-stop via Market Drayton to Crewe. The Birkenhead portion would leave Wolverhampton seven minutes later.

Shrewsbury and Chester: Gobowen station is seen in the 1950s when it was still a significant stop on a main line to London. Castle 5061 Earl of Birkenhead is appropriately at the head of what is probably a Birkenhead to Paddington train.
RUSSELL MULFORD

It would appear from the timetable that local travellers were not of any great importance to the GWR. For example, if one wished to travel from Albrighton to Shrewsbury, the first train to call was the 7.33am, but it only ran as far as Wellington. After waiting there for twenty-eight minutes, a Stafford to Shrewsbury train would call, arriving at Shrewsbury at 8.53am. The next westbound train from Albrighton was the 10.36am (to Shrewsbury, arriving 11.40am) and after that, the 12.39 (again, only to Wellington).

Similarly, Baschurch, some 8 miles (13km) north of Shrewsbury, saw just six northbound trains per day, one more than the smaller stations such as Leaton, or Rednal and West Felton.

On Sundays, just five trains were scheduled to run from Wolverhampton to Shrewsbury. The 11.10am from Paddington, a 'Birmingham and the North Express', offered a 'Luncheon and Tea Car to Shrewsbury' and ran to a schedule almost an hour slower than the best weekday service. The fifth northbound train was the 6.00pm from Paddington, which terminated at Shrewsbury.

Oswestry, on the Shrewsbury and Chester's branch line from Gobowen, was served by twenty-three shuttle trains that ran in each direction every weekday (twenty-four on Wednesdays).

Crewe to Hereford

The North and West was not a radial route from London; nevertheless it was a major route – in every respect a main line. It is worth remembering the pattern of railway ownership before the grouping – routes that appear today to be natural were not necessarily so in 1922. The direct railway route from Birmingham to Bristol was operated by the Midland Railway; for trains originating in north-west England, the North and West had since 1886 provided an alternative, via Maindee Junction (Newport) and the Severn Tunnel.

Pages 450 to 451 of the July 1922 *Bradshaw's* bear the title 'Crewe, Chester, Whitchurch, Shrewsbury, Craven Arms, and Hereford – L&NW and GW'. The clue as to the route's importance lies in the starting points and destinations of the trains and through carriages: to the north, these are Glasgow (Central), Edinburgh (Princes Street), Carlisle, Leeds (New), Liverpool (Lime Street) and Manchester (London Road). Beyond Hereford, destinations are Pontypool Road, Newport, Cardiff, Bristol, Exeter (St David's) and Plymouth (Millbay).

The first southbound train of the day (except Mondays) would leave Crewe at 1.25am and arrive at Shrewsbury at 2.13am. There it would split, the first portion leaving at 2.25am, bound for South

The joint Shrewsbury and Birmingham/Shropshire Union Wellington station, summer 1960: the 7.10am Pwllheli to Paddington (Saturdays only) was not scheduled to call, so it is on the through road. 7817 Garsington Manor was shedded at Croes Newydd (Wrexham): the train will have run non-stop along the former GWR line through Dolgellau and Llangollen and 7817 will have been attached when the train reversed at Ruabon. RUSSELL MULFORD

Shrewsbury and Hereford, near Bayston Hill: the building on the right is a former S&H signal cabin, long disused when the relatively modern 1003 County of Wilts passed with a North and West train in 1955.
RUSSELL MULFORD

Wales (the 'North and South Wales Express' to Newport and Cardiff); fifteen minutes later, the second portion ('North and West Express') would pull out, heading for Bristol, Exeter and Plymouth. Bradshaw advises 'Through Carriages, except on Saturdays, Aberdeen to Plymouth and Glasgow to Exeter, via Carlisle and Severn Tunnel'.

Five more 'North and West Expresses' would pass down the line during the course of the day, arriving at Shrewsbury at 11.20am ('Luncheon and Tea Car, Liverpool (L St) to Plymouth'), 12.27pm ('Luncheon, Tea and Dining Car' as per the 11.20), 1.55pm ('Luncheon and Tea Car, Liverpool (L St) to Taunton'), 4.47pm ('Through Carriage. Glasgow to Plymouth') and 9.12pm.

Numerous 'locals' or stopping trains also ran up and down the line. Some, running from Crewe, would terminate at Shrewsbury, while others would start at Shrewsbury and run to Hereford. LNWR Swansea trains would also run, non-stop, between Shrewsbury and Craven Arms. Relatively few 'stoppers' ran through Shrewsbury along the full length of the route.

Sunday services were sparse. Again, a 2.13am arrival from the north would split at Shrewsbury, into a 'North and South Wales Express' and a 'North and West Express'. At 3.40am, a train departed for Hereford, stopping at Craven Arms, Ludlow and Leominster. Another 'North and West Express' paused shortly after midday, at 12.32pm. Lastly, a 'stopper' left Crewe at midday, and arrived at the county town at 1.15pm. This service continued at 5.20pm, with a leisurely run to Hereford. Calling at some, but not all stations, it arrived at Hereford at 7.08pm.

Shropshire's only water troughs were on the North and West, at Bromfield, just to the north of Ludlow. Unrebuilt Patriot no. 45520 Llandudno heads south with an eleven-coach train on 1 September 1956. RUSSELL MULFORD

Central Wales Line

The LNWR's route to South Wales, from Craven Arms to Swansea, was considered a main line, so its passenger service, although fairly sparse, had the characteristics of services on the GWR main line and the North and West. It had 'stoppers' and 'semi-fast' trains – hardly an express, the fastest southbound train was the 2.40pm from Shrewsbury, scheduled to arrive in Swansea at 6.58pm, an average speed of almost 26mph (42km/h). Trains to and from Swansea conveyed through carriages serving a number of places well beyond Shrewsbury. Some trains ran just part way along the line.

Other than the 3.30pm to Knighton, trains did not generally start out from Craven Arms. First train of the day was the 3.30am from Shrewsbury, with through carriages from York. It was followed by through trains to Swansea at 6.30am, 11.45am, 12.50pm – 'Through Carriages, Liverpool (Lime St.) to Swansea (Victoria) and Manchester (London Road) to Pembroke Dock' – 2.40pm and 5.10pm. The 5.10pm conveyed through carriages from Liverpool and Manchester, the 2.40pm conveyed 'Thro' Carrs., Liverpool & Manchester to Swansea (Vic.) & Birmingham to Central Wales Spas', as well as a through carriage from London Euston to the same destinations. Clearly, the Central Wales was a main line.

The Cambrian

One other main line ran through Shropshire – that of the Cambrian Railways, from Whitchurch to Aberystwyth. Although the LNWR had long been the Cambrian's 'preferred partner', it had been absorbed by the GWR, in anticipation of the grouping, from 1 January 1922. As a result, the service – 'Whitchurch, Oswestry, Welshpool and Aberystwyth' – is shown on pages 578 to 581 as 'G.W. (late Cambrian)'.

Thirteen trains were due to leave Oswestry southbound on weekdays, though the pattern of these services is not simple. Not all trains ran every day, nor did they all run the full length of the main line. On Mondays to Fridays, the last train was the 6.50pm from Whitchurch, which left Oswestry at

7.45pm and terminated at Welshpool at 8.25pm. But on Saturdays only, a train would start from Oswestry at 9.30pm (connections from Manchester and Liverpool, departing 6.30pm and 6.20pm respectively), to run all stations to Four Crosses, just 7½ miles (12km) to the south.

The day's first train left Whitchurch at 2.45am and was scheduled to run to Aberystwyth, some 95¾ miles (154km) away, in just under four hours. Averaging below 25mph (40km/h), nevertheless it made few stops in the early part of its run, calling en route at Ellesmere, Oswestry, Llanymynech and Welshpool. Stops would be more frequent as the hour became more reasonable.

The next train south from Whitchurch would leave at 8.15am, calling at all stations, to terminate at Oswestry at 9.05am. At the same time as that train left Whitchurch, a train left Oswestry to run all stations ('Arddleen: stops on Mondays only; Talerddig: stops when required') to Aberystwyth.

The second train to run the full length of the main line left Whitchurch at 10.00am. Advertised as 'Through Train, Birmingham (Snow Hill) to Aberystwyth, Through Train, Birkenhead to Aberystwyth', the Snow Hill portion is the 'Aberystwyth Express' mentioned above. The Birkenhead portion is advertised on page 87 as a 'Through Carriage, Birkenhead to Aberystwyth' on the 9.05am 'Birkenhead, Birmingham and Leamington Spa Express' to Paddington.

Just three more trains ran the full length of the main line, leaving Whitchurch at 1.50pm, 2.05pm and 4.05pm. The 1.50pm, due in Aberystwyth at 5.15pm, was an express, advertised as a through train from Birkenhead to Aberystwyth, with 'Through Carriages, London (Euston), Birmingham (New Street) to Aberystwyth'. The 2.05pm was an all-stations 'stopper', while the 4.05pm, which stopped at most, but not all, stations, conveyed (from Welshpool) a 'Through Carriage, London (Paddington) to Aberystwyth'.

There was just one train in each direction on Sundays. The 2.35pm from Whitchurch would arrive in Oswestry at 3.20pm, where it would remain until 6.40pm, when it continued its journey to the

At Shropshire's northern extremity on the Crewe line, 40529 is an interloper, having been built for the LNWR's rival, the Midland Railway, in 1898. No longer in top link service, it had no more than two years' service ahead when it worked this Chester train at Whitchurch in 1952.
RUSSELL MULFORD

Welsh coast, arriving in Aberystwyth at 9.25pm. By definition, it was a through train, although it is hard to imagine many passengers using it as such.

Tanat Valley: Three passenger trains per day ran up the valley from Oswestry to the terminus at Llangynog, weekdays only. The 8.10am ran every day, taking an hour and ten minutes for the 19½-mile (30.5km) journey. The 11.35am and the 4.20pm ran every day apart from Wednesdays and Saturdays, when they ran at 2.15pm and 4.50pm respectively. A fourth train 'Runs on the 1st Wednesday in the month' at 8.00pm.

Llanfyllin: Shropshire's Llanymynech was the junction for the Llanfyllin branch. Five trains ran up the Cain Valley on weekdays – two starting from Oswestry, the others from Llanymynech, with a sixth train on Saturdays only.

Stafford to Welshpool

Not perhaps an obvious through route, the line did see some through services between the extremities, as well as longer-distance trains between London and the Welsh coast. Purely LNWR between Stafford and Wellington, the route is then GWR and LNWR joint to Buttington Junction, near Welshpool. Notwithstanding the need to reverse in Shrewsbury (assuming trains were intended to stop there), the route is encapsulated on page 461 of the 1922 *Bradshaw's Guide* – as 'Stafford, Newport, Wellington, Shrewsbury and Welshpool – L.N.W. and G.W.'.

The first train each weekday ('Except Mondays'), the 1.55am from Stafford, was a through train, stopping only at Newport, Wellington and Shrewsbury en route. The 'normal' service from Stafford to Shrewsbury consisted of ten weekday trains, stopping (apart from the 8.50am from Stafford) at all stations to Wellington. The 8.50am omitted Haughton (near Stafford), Trench Crossing and Hadley. Only the first 'stopper', the 7.25am from Stafford, deigned to call at Admaston, Walcot and Upton Magna. The last train of the day left Stafford at 10.00pm, terminating at Shrewsbury at 11.09pm.

Most trains from Stafford terminated at Shrewsbury – but not all. The 5.20pm and 8.13pm ran through to Welshpool, stopping at all stations along that line. At 1.35pm, a train left Stafford and ran non-stop to Shrewsbury. Reversing there, it would then run non-stop to Welshpool. Conveying 'Through carriages, London (Euston) and

Birmingham (New Street) to Aberystwyth', this was the train mentioned under 'The Cambrian' (above), arriving at the Welsh terminus at 5.15pm.

Between Shrewsbury and Welshpool, the local train service commenced with the 7.45am to Welshpool, a GWR train that had started out from Birmingham at 6.00am. Just five locals ran in each direction. The next two were also GWR trains, the 10.25am and the 2.45pm from Shrewsbury, both originating at Snow Hill. The last locals were the two from Stafford, mentioned above. There were also the non-stop trains, already mentioned, running from Paddington and London Euston to the Welsh coast.

The Sunday service only ran between Stafford and Shrewsbury, consisting of just one train in each direction.

Minsterley: The branch commenced at Cruckmeole Junction, about half a mile (800m) beyond Hanwood station, which was also served by branch trains. Six trains ran every weekday (eight on Saturdays), typically taking thirty minutes for the 10-mile (16km) trip. There was a Sunday service – a 7.45pm departure from Shrewsbury, which stayed in Minsterley just thirty-five minutes before returning to Shrewsbury.

Coalport: Coalport was still the home of the eponymous china in 1922 – manufacture moved to Staffordshire four years later. The train service was pretty straightforward – five per day, plus a sixth on Saturdays, which only ran between Wellington and Oakengates. There were no trains on Sundays. First train from Coalport was the 6.50am to Wellington; the first to Coalport left Wellington at 8.05am (it was probably of little use to the china workers) and the day's last train arrived at Coalport at 9.44pm, running half an hour later on Saturdays. Trains were allowed thirty-three minutes for their 9½ mile (15km) run.

Severn Valley: Most trains ran to and from Worcester, a journey of some 52 miles (84km). South of Bewdley, the timetable was not completely straightforward, but for the 35¼ miles (56.7km) between Shrewsbury and Bewdley, the service is easy to describe. A total of five trains left the county town, at 8.10am, 11.25am, 1.50pm, 5.30pm

and 7.40pm. Similarly, five ran northwards from Bewdley to Shrewsbury. These trains called at all stations, taking, at best, about an hour and a half, including usually a five-minute stop at Bridgnorth. An early morning train ('Motor Car, one class only') ran from Kidderminster to Highley and back. Arriving at Highley at 5.56am, it returned some eleven minutes later. Another 'Motor Car' train left Bewdley at 8.18pm for Bridgnorth. Taking thirty minutes for the run, it returned southwards at 8.55pm. There was no Sunday service.

Wellington to Crewe: Six 'stoppers' ran northwards from Wellington through to Crewe (using the GWR's running powers on the LNWR line from Nantwich); curiously, only five ran in the opposite direction, plus an 8.10pm Crewe to Market Drayton train, last of the day. The extra train northwards may be accounted for by the 11.46am from Wellington, which is advertised as a 'Through train, Worcester to Crewe'. Shortly after this train, a non-stop run from Wellington to Crewe followed – the 'Bournemouth and Manchester Express'. Its southbound counterpart, the 11.05am from Crewe, did not stop anywhere on the line, but is nevertheless included in Bradshaw's table.

On Sundays, the 10.45am from Crewe took an hour and a half for the 32-mile (51km) journey to Wellington; the slightly quicker 5.40pm train from Wellington arrived at Crewe at 7.05pm.

Market Drayton to Stoke: The town famed for its gingerbread was well-served in 1922. As well as its services to Crewe and Wellington, there were six trains on the North Staffordshire line to and from Stoke each weekday (with an extra train to Market Drayton on market day, Wednesday, and an extra train to Stoke on Saturdays). Two trains ran each way on Sundays – the 9.00am from Stoke, returning from Market Drayton at 10.06am, and the 7.30pm from Market Drayton, with a return working from Stoke at 8.55pm.

Wellington to Craven Arms: The service was pretty sparse, even in 1922. Six trains per day ran in each direction between Wellington and Much Wenlock, plus an unbalanced 6.30am from Coalbrookdale to Wellington, the first northbound

The last few yards of the Severn Valley line as it approaches Sutton Bridge Junction. GWR 2-6-2T no. 4105 passes the remains of the former carriage shed on left; in the background can be seen the bridge carrying the Shropshire and Montgomeryshire Railway towards Abbey Station. It was still in use when this picture was taken in 1954. RUSSELL MULFORD

train each day. However, only three trains per day ran between Much Wenlock and Craven Arms. The first southbound train started from Much Wenlock, at 6.50am; the others ran from Wellington. The shortest working was the 6.20pm, from Much Wenlock (last northbound train of the day) to Buildwas Junction. Returning south at 6.36pm, it was allowed twelve minutes for the 3¼ miles (5km) at 1 in 40.

All trains called at all stations – apart from the 6.30am from Much Wenlock, which omitted the stop at Harton Road. Who knows why? There was no Sunday service on the line.

Woofferton to Kidderminster: Five trains ran in each direction along the full 24¼ miles (39km) of the route, via Tenbury Wells, Cleobury Mortimer and Bewdley. Fastest train of the day was the first westbound, taking just one hour and four minutes. It was scheduled to stand at Tenbury for six minutes. Slower schedules were usually the result of longer stops here and at Bewdley, where they would connect with Severn Valley services.

In addition to the through trains, there were five westbound and six eastbound trains on the joint line between Woofferton and Tenbury.

Wellington to Much Wenlock line: a GWR steam railcar is seen in action, probably in the early years of the twentieth century. IRONBRIDGE GORGE MUSEUM TRUST

CHAPTER 3

GWR and LMS

The Grouping

On 1 January 1923, Britain's railways entered a new phase. Lasting just twenty-five years, in many ways it defined the British railway of the twentieth century. In order to serve the needs of the nation during World War I, the railways were taken under state control. That control remained in place until 1921, by which time the next step was under serious consideration by Parliament. The benefits of a more rational organization had become clear. Full nationalization was considered, but the benefits of competition would then be lost.

The outcome, the Railways Act 1921, provided for combination of the pre-grouping companies,

more than 100, into what became known as 'the Big Four'. A number of amalgamations took place in 1922, in the run-up to 1 January 1923, when 'The Grouping' took effect. The London and North Eastern Railway (LNER) is outside the scope of this book, although some of its tentacles, such as the Great Central's lines in the Wrexham area, came close to the county. Similarly, the Southern Railway (SR) can be dismissed. The other two new companies were the London, Midland and Scottish (LMS), and the Great Western Railway (GWR).

The LMS, LNER and SR each included a number of the larger pre-grouping companies. The LMS brought together major companies such as the London and North Western (the self-styled

The Cambrian is now part of the GWR: 0-6-0 no. 898, formerly CR no. 14, is seen in Oswestry station with a goods train on 23 April 1939. Built by Sharp, Stewart in 1875, it survived the war, but was withdrawn from service in 1947. A.N.H. GLOVER/ KIDDERMINSTER RAILWAY MUSEUM

'Premier Line'), the Midland and the Lancashire and Yorkshire, as well as some smaller players such as the North Staffordshire, plus some Scottish companies. It is thought to have been, for a short while, the world's largest joint stock company.

The pre-grouping GWR became, in effect, a greater Great Western. It was, by route mileage (around 3,000 miles [4,800km]) the biggest pre-grouping company; none of its acquisitions had a network as big as a tenth of that size, although the intensity of traffic carried by some of the South Wales companies, such as the Taff Vale, makes route mileage a poor comparator. Most of the GWR's acquisitions were in fact South Wales companies; it also gained the Cambrian Railways. By route mileage it was the second biggest constituent of the enlarged GWR, but contributed just ninety-four standard-gauge locomotives.

Before the grouping, two major companies had ruled Shropshire's rails. After the grouping, little had changed. The only differences were at the periphery. In the north-east, that short stretch of North Staffs running into Market Drayton was now part of the LMS. In the west, the Cambrian Railways were now Great Western. The joint lines remained under the control of Shrewsbury's Joint Superintendent until 1932. From that year, the station and joint network came under the operational control of the GWR, though the LMS continued to use the lines as before. At the same time, Chester station, and lines to the north of it, came under LMS control.

What Might Have Been

Britain's railway network was more or less complete by the start of World War I. New construction had slowed to a trickle by that date; after the war, one of the very last new railway lines to be built was the Wolverhampton and Kingswinford Railway. Opened in 1925, it was more usually known as the Kingswinford branch, or, after the large (supposedly England's largest) village it served, the Wombourne branch. It may be that this period marks the true zenith of railways in the UK, for, just seven years later, the line was closed to passengers, though it remained open for freight. Its significance to Shropshire's railways is twofold.

Firstly, for forty years the line provided a useful goods route around the western perimeter of the busy Birmingham and Black Country conurbation. A northbound train would join the line at Kingswinford junction, Brettell Lane, between Stourbridge and Brierley Hill. At the northern end of the line, it would take the south to west side of the triangular Oxley Junction and continue into Shropshire along the GWR main line. At Wellington, it could either run via Shrewsbury to Chester and Birkenhead, or take the Market Drayton line to Crewe. Gradual freight decline led to closure in 1965.

The second significance of the Kingswinford branch lies in plans prepared by the GWR in the early years of the twentieth century, for a railway from Wombourne to Bridgnorth and the Severn Valley line. Crossing the Severn near Quatt, there would have been a triangular junction near Eardington, south of Bridgnorth. It appears that some staking out of the route took place, plus some minor earthworks near Eardington's Crossing Cottage, but nothing more came of the scheme. Although there is significant commuter traffic from Bridgnorth to Wolverhampton and the West Midlands, it is hard to imagine that such a rural line could have survived much longer than the ill-fated Kingswinford branch.

The Halts

Despite the failure of the Wombourne branch, the GWR continued to expand, after a fashion, in Shropshire and elsewhere. During the 1930s, facing growing road competition for passenger traffic, the company opened numerous halts. These unstaffed minimal stations typically comprised a wooden shelter and a short wooden platform. A hand signal from the platform or prior notice to the guard was needed to stop the train. Those opened within the county include:

Shrewsbury to Chester: Oldwoods, Stanwardine, Haughton and Trehowell. Park Hall, on the Gobowen to Oswestry branch, appears to be the county's first halt. Opened in 1926, it served the Shropshire Orthopaedic Hospital, which had been established on the site of Park Hall Camp hospital, a World War I military facility.

Shrewsbury to Wolverhampton: New Hadley. Admaston was downgraded to halt status by BR in 1952.

Shrewsbury to Hereford: All Stretton, Little Stretton, Wistanstow.

Shrewsbury to Welshpool: Plas-y-Court.

Shrewsbury to Bewdley: Cound, Jackfield, Alveley. The latter, not shown on public timetables, opened as 'Alveley Colliery Sidings', after the mine that began production in 1937. It was later known as Alveley Colliery Halt and finally just Alveley Halt. Eardington station, between Bridgnorth and Hampton Loade, opened with the railway, but was demoted to a halt towards the end of its life.

Wellington to Nantwich: Longden, Rowton, Ellerdine, Wollerton – and Little Drayton, which only lasted until 1941.

Wellington to Craven Arms: Ketley Town, New Dale, Doseley, Green Bank, Farley, Westwood, Easthope.

The actual dates of opening appear randomly scattered through those years. No two halts seem to have opened on the same day. The last to open in Shropshire as a new facility (as opposed a down-grading of an existing station) was probably Tinkers Green Halt, on the former Cambrian line about 1 mile (1.6km) north-east of Oswestry station. Like Park Hall Halt, it was opened to serve the military training camp at Park Hall, in October 1939. Most of the halts had short lives, remaining in use until

Little Stretton Halt was opened by the GWR on 18 April 1935. Along with near neighbour All Stretton, it was temporarily closed from January 1943, reopening in May 1946. It lasted a further twelve years, closing permanently in June 1958, along with other halts and lesser stations on the line. It does not look as though this Castle-hauled train was intending to stop. RUSSELL MULFORD

Cosford's wooden station was opened in 1937 to serve the nearby RAF base. On 15 April 1981, it evidently continued to serve that purpose. Passengers prepare to board a Wolverhampton-bound service provided by a former Western Region class 120 DMU.

either the line was closed, or local stopping services were withdrawn from the line. None remains within the county, though the former Birches and Bilbrook Halt, near Codsall, dating from 1934, is still open. It was renamed 'Bilbrook' in 1974. Between Wellington and Oakengates, the 1934 New Hadley Halt survived until 1986.

Halts were the GWR's lowest tier of passenger facility. Somewhere between 'halt' and 'station' was the designation 'platform'. Lightmoor Platform, dating from 1907, was for a time blessed with a pair of 'pagodas', curious and typically GWR corrugated iron structures, with oriental-looking roofs. Providing lockable storage, more than was required by a halt, pagodas were widely seen across the GWR.

Locomotives: GWR

At the start of the 'Big Four' period, there were few major changes to the locomotives used in and around the county. From the Great Western standpoint, little had changed, not even the company name. GWR locomotives continued to be recognizably such – though there were changes.

Probably the most significant development was the introduction of the Castle Class 4-cylinder 4–6–0 during the first year of the grouping. A development of the 1907 Star Class, a small number of Stars were actually rebuilt as Castles. Certainly one of the most successful steam classes to be built in the UK, their construction continued until the last of 171 appeared in 1950, in BR days. They would become a familiar sight in Shropshire, on the main-line expresses between Wolverhampton and Birkenhead and on the North and West through to Hereford and Bristol. Elsewhere on the GWR, the Castles were displaced from the heaviest expresses by the larger King Class locomotives, thirty of which were introduced from 1927. Because of weight restrictions, the Kings were not allowed on the lines to Shrewsbury in GWR days.

The first 4–6–0s to be allocated to Shrewsbury were the 2-cylindered Saints, predecessors of the 'Halls', shortly before World War I. From 1930, Stars began to replace them, with no fewer than eleven being allocated in the early 1930s. Shrewsbury's

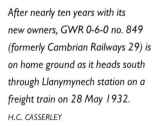

After nearly ten years with its new owners, GWR 0-6-0 no. 849 (formerly Cambrian Railways 29) is on home ground as it heads south through Llanymynech station on a freight train on 28 May 1932.
H.C. CASSERLEY

5034 Corfe Castle, built in 1935, is about to stop at Wellington with a north-bound train in 1958. To the right are the lines to bay platforms 1 and 2, still in use for Much Wenlock trains. RUSSELL MULFORD

first Castles were allocated in 1934 – the last of the Saints disappeared soon afterwards and the Stars slowly faded, though some lasted to BR days.

GWR 4–4–0s could also be seen throughout the period. Some of the older locomotives were used on stopping trains on the main lines, while in 1936 a 'new' 4–4–0 class appeared. The 'Dukedogs', as they were generally but unofficially known, were in effect an amalgam of two older types – a Duke type boiler on Bulldog frames. Their low axle loading meant they could operate on the former Cambrian lines, on which they were widely used, being one of just a small number of classes permitted on the wooden Barmouth Bridge.

The last truly new GWR 4–4–0 design was the County Class, which appeared in 1904. In effect they were shortened Saints, with two rather than three driving axles. Unlike the earlier 4–4–0s, they were outside-cylindered and inside-framed, a much more modern-looking design. One of their intended routes was the Hereford to Shrewsbury line, on which at that time the 4–6–0s were forbidden. Notoriously rough-riding, they had all gone by 1933. Twelve years later, a new County Class locomotive emerged from Swindon – the GWR's last new 4–6–0 design. Thirty were built between 1945 and 1947 and by the end of the GWR's life could be seen running between Wolverhampton and Chester. Like the previous County Class, they pushed the design threshold a little. They had 2 outside cylinders – unlike the Stars, Castles and Kings, there were no inside cylinders to deal with, though the valve gear remained stubbornly inside the frames. Neater than the tangle of Walschaerts outside valve gear on their LMS counterparts at Coleham, it was less easy to maintain. Less obvious was their 280psi boiler pressure (later reduced to 250psi) – until the safety valves blew …

The smallest 4–6–0s were the popular Manors, introduced in 1938, which saw extensive use on the former Cambrian lines well into the BR period. As well as Shrewsbury, a number were allocated

Sunlight streams through the glazing of the overall roof as 'Dukedog' no. 9013 pilots the Cambrian Coast Express into Shrewsbury station in 1952. The south-end footbridge, which was removed at the same time as the roof in the early 1960s, can clearly be seen at the end of the platform. RUSSELL MULFORD

Wellington locomotive shed, beside the station, is seen in the 1930s. The precise date is not known, but 2-6-2T no. 5189, on the right, was built in 1929; on the left is no. 3222, a Dean Barnum 2-4-0. They had all gone by early 1937. PHOTOGRAPHER UNKNOWN/ KIDDERMINSTER RAILWAY MUSEUM

to Oswestry, where they lived alongside their dwindling former Cambrian colleagues. Several Cambrian classes lived on throughout the period into BR days, though their appearance was 'Great-Westernized' over the years.

Most types of GWR locomotive, such as the Grange and Hall 4-6-0s, would be seen at Shrewsbury. Inevitably, the pannier and prairie tanks appeared on the branch lines. The 44XX 2-6-2Ts were allocated to Much Wenlock from July 1934, replacing earlier 0-4-2Ts. Some of the more unusual residents at Shrewsbury shed included members of the 3000 Class 2-8-0 locomotives of Great Central design. Built for World War I service, 100 were bought by the GWR afterwards. Their GWR counterparts, members of the 2800 and 2884 Classes, were not often resident, though would pass through the county on freight.

SHROPSHIRE RAILWAYMEN – JOE POWELL

The late Joe Powell started with the GWR in 1930, working his way up to driver in time-honoured fashion. His son Charlie relates stories of steam days as told by father.

As a young fireman, Joe learned greatly from senior drivers, 'true craftsmen' in his eyes. Once, passing the sheds at Coleham with a fully loaded passenger train, the driver set the regulator and cut-off and said 'Watch this, I'll not touch this engine again until Stretton and given a clear road we'll pass on time', which of course they did. Heading south, a Salop fireman would be fresh, at the beginning of his day's work, but it would be different in the opposite direction. The climb might be easier, but the shift could have started in Devon ... Joe liked to see them 'go' on the descent towards home, but you had to hold on tight through the reverse curves at Micklewood ('especially on an LMS engine'). Goods trains, however, needed to be kept in check down the bank: if not fully controlled by Bayston Hill, a freight might run away through Shrewsbury station, which did happen on occasion.

Hencote bank on the Chester line was another hard climb out of town, especially when starting a heavy goods train from Coton Hill sidings, but it could be useful. Joe once relieved the crew of a 'Hall' at Shrewsbury station. On a Chester passenger working, the loco was not in the best of condition and the fire was 'a terrible mess'.

They did their best to clean the fire while standing, but it was not until the locomotive was working hard up the bank and 'draughting' the fire that they were able to get the boiler pressure 'up to the mark'. They arrived in Chester on time. Goods trains down the bank again had to be kept in check. Towards the end of Joe's career, a runaway down the bank led to the Coton Hill crash. It happened on a Monday morning, Joe's rest day – it was to have been his rostered turn for the rest of that week.

In the Paddington direction there was quite a climb through Wellington to Hollinswood. The London expresses could make a tremendous sound as they passed under Shrewsbury's Monkmoor Road. A friend who lived nearby watched Joe go past rather steadily one day. When they next met, he said 'You'll have to give it more than that or you'll lose time.' Joe took no notice. 'There's no need to work the engine too hard. Look towards the next over-bridge and you will see a hump. The line then dips down to Belvidere Bridge across the Severn. You can pick up plenty speed there before starting to climb to Upton Magna, and of course you're keeping your fireman happy.' Approaching Belvidere from the east, with a goods train, he would apply a little brake to get them 'all buffered up', judging his speed so that the train would push them over the same hump in controlled fashion for a smooth approach to town.

In the early years of the LMS, 195 compound 4-4-0s were built to a Midland Railway design. BR no. 41159 dated from 1925 and it was withdrawn in 1958. The diamond-shaped works plate indicates that it was built by the North British Locomotive Company in Glasgow. The locomotive is seen in the mid-1950s on the turntable at Shrewsbury shed (LMS side). *RUSSELL MULFORD*

Locomotives: LMS

The twenty-five-year life of the LMS can be split into two periods – before and after Stanier. Joining the LMS in 1932 from Swindon, where he was works manager, William Stanier revolutionized the company's motive power. Before his reign began, locomotives of the former LNWR were still heavily relied upon in Shropshire, especially on local passenger and freight, though 'foreigners' and early LMS types began to appear. The LNWR Prince of Wales Class 4–6–0 locomotives, built from 1912 to 1921, would be seen on the North and West

Expresses between Shrewsbury and Crewe, beginning to share their duties with the Midland/LMS compounds.

The Stafford line was not in the same league as the Crewe line – here, the smaller 4–4–0s of the Precursor and George the Fifth Classes might seen.

Henry Fowler, Chief Mechanical Engineer of the LMS from 1925 to 1931, was a 'small engine' man – hence the compound 4–4–0s mentioned above – but he was responsible for some more substantial locomotives, such as the Crabs. These powerful but ungainly looking 2–6–0s were designed by his

Standing under the gantry at Shrewsbury in the mid-1950s with a North and West train, 45500 Patriot was the first of a class of fifty 'new' 4-6-0 locomotives built by the LMS. Nominally (for accounting reasons) rebuilds of LNWR Claughton 4-6-0s, LMS nos. 5500 and 5501 incorporated some parts of the originals (visibly the large centre bosses of the driving wheels), but to all intents and purposes they were new locomotives. Eighteen were further rebuilt between 1946 and 1948; 45500 remained in original condition and all were withdrawn between 1960 and 1965. *RUSSELL MULFORD*

Stanier Black Five 45143 stops at Craven Arms with a southbound service in 1962, when trains still ran to Swansea (Victoria).
RUSSELL MULFORD

predecessor, Hughes. Fowler put 245 locomotives into service and they spread to all parts of the LMS system. His 2–6–4 tanks, though clearly of the same family, were more elegant in appearance and were well-used on the Central Wales line passenger services, where they took on the work of LNWR locomotives such as the 4–6–2Ts dating from 1910.

Many smaller ex-LNWR locomotives, such as the Cauliflowers and Coal Tanks, could be usefully employed around the county. The coal tanks saw out passenger services to (appropriately) Coalport and the long-lived 0–8–0 freight locomotives also trundled their freights up and down the North and West into BR days.

Notwithstanding the arrival of the Royal Scot (1927) and Patriot (1930) Class 4–6–0s, the LMS scene changed, almost beyond recognition, when Stanier arrived. Charged with modernizing and enlarging LMS locomotives, he did just that. His 4–6–0 Black Five in particular was hugely success-ful. Dating from 1934, 842 were built and the class saw out steam on British Rail in 1968. The mixed-traffic design was used all over the LMS system, as

was the 8F 2–8–0 freight locomotive. 852 of these were built, though not all saw service in the UK – many were built for wartime service overseas and some never returned.

Stanier's masterpieces were his Pacifics – the Princess Royal and the Coronation Classes. Intended for, and used on, the west coast main line between London Euston and Glasgow, they would appear fairly frequently at Shrewsbury, often ex-works on running-in turns. Unlike the various 4–6–0 types, they did not tend to venture any further south. The North and West Expresses, LMS-hauled from Crewe, would change engines at Shrewsbury – a copper-capped chimney would adorn the loco-motive south of the county town.

Streamlined LMS Coronation Pacific no. 6225 Duchess of Gloucester is seen at the north end of Shrewsbury station in 1938. They were a fairly common sight on test trips from Crewe works. RailPhotoprints.co.uk
COLLECTION

CHAPTER 4

British Railways 1948–1994

Nationalization

The 'Big Four' were in effect a consequence of World War I. Just twenty-five years later, after another world war, they passed into history. On 1 January 1948, they were taken into public ownership as a part of the Railway Executive of the British Transport Commission. Trading as 'British Railways', this title was abbreviated to 'British Rail' in 1965.

Once again, they had been run, during the war, as a single entity. Intensive use of the network had been essential; investment and maintenance fell by the wayside. Restoring the railways to pre-war condition would incur huge costs that the companies would have struggled to fund. There might have been other ways in which money could have been injected, but one objective of the post-war Labour Government was the 'common ownership of the means of production, distribution and exchange'. As with, for example, coal, electricity and gas, the airways and the Bank of England, nationalization was the future. Significantly, after the Conservatives came to power in 1951, only road transport and the most recently nationalized steel industry were returned to private ownership.

The Regions

British Railways would not be monolithic – the railways were to be organized on a regional basis. Scotland's railways became the Scottish Region; having in effect lost the 'S', former LMS lines in England and Wales were designated 'London Midland Region'. The new 'Western Region' occupied the former GWR's lines. There were exceptions, such as the former LMS route from Craven Arms to Swansea, which became part of the Western Region (but continued to use LMS locomotives and stock). Inevitably, the joint nature of much of Shropshire's network meant that there would be some blurring of distinction in the county. New signage began to appear, including the now-classic enamel 'hot dog' station signs in regional colours – maroon for the London Midland and brown for the Western (echoing the old companies' coach liveries).

The regions were reorganized in 1963, when the former GWR main line north of Birmingham and Shrewsbury, along with all former Western Region lines north of Craven Arms, became part of the Chester Division of the London Midland Region. Three years later, a further reorganization placed Shrewsbury within the Stoke Division.

Early Closures

Road competition had begun to hit the railways after World War I, when thousands of war-surplus vehicles became available. The railways had long held the status of 'Common Carrier'. A nineteenth-century measure aimed at preventing railway companies from 'cherry-picking', it now enabled road hauliers to do just that. The railways were left to carry traffic that the roads did not want, often at unprofitable rates. Freight rates for profitable traffic had to be sufficient to cross-subsidize those losses and were inevitably undercut by the roads. From 1953, the legislation was relaxed, but the damage had been done. For much traffic, road haulage was simpler, cheaper and quicker.

Passenger traffic dwindled too, from around 1,000 million passenger journeys per year at nationalization, to 630 million in 1982. Car ownership increased, especially after petrol rationing ended in 1953. Competition from the airways began to affect long-distance routes and while the numbers might not be huge, the image was altogether more modern. Passenger trains were old-fashioned and, in steam days, dirty.

The first thirty-five years of the BR period were characterized by decline of traffic and with that decline came closures. The network had eventually extended to around 21,000 route miles (34,000km); today it is nearer 10,000 miles (16,500km).

Closures tend to be associated with the Beeching era; in fact, they had begun (not to any significant extent) before World War II. In 1949, the British Transport Commission formed a 'Branch Lines Committee', whose brief was to close the least-used parts of the network: more than 3,000 miles (4,800km) were closed as a result in the pre-'Beeching Report' years. The case for those lines was not helped by coal shortages. Despite the conversion of a small number of locomotives to oil-firing, service suspension and closure soon took effect: four Shropshire lines were involved in the first round of closures, and others followed when the financial position worsened from the mid-1950s.

Tanat Valley

Shropshire's first post-nationalization passenger closure took effect from 15 January 1951, when the service from Oswestry to Llangynog was withdrawn temporarily due to the coal shortage; within days, it was announced that the withdrawal would become permanent from 5 February. Of the stations closed, the first four, travelling from Oswestry, were in Shropshire: Porthywaen; Blodwell Junction; Llanyblodwell; and, some 8 miles (13km) from Oswestry, Glanyrafon. Freight to Llangynog ended some eighteen months later, but continued to Llanrhaiadr Mochnant until 1960, when floods damaged a bridge. The last Tanat Valley metals to carry traffic, from Porthywaen to Nantmawr Junction, remained in use until 1988, when Blodwell Quarry closed. Those rails are still in place and may one day see passenger trains again, operated by the Cambrian Heritage Railways preservationists.

Minsterley

On the same day that the Tanat Valley closure became permanent, 5 February 1951, the Minsterley branch passenger service also ended. There had been three trains per day in 1949, working from Shrewsbury to Minsterley and back. The 8.05am from Minsterley, arriving in Shrewsbury at 8.31am, might have suited some commuters, but the last train home left the county town at 6.20pm – rather late for homebound office workers, but far too early for an evening in town. Freight continued into the mid-1960s, finally succumbing on 1 May 1967. The line remained available for the testing of Shrewsbury-built Sentinel/Rolls-Royce diesels until 1973, when locomotive production moved to the Rotherham factory of Thomas Hill.

Much Wenlock to Craven Arms

The passenger service south from Much Wenlock ended on the last day of 1951. South of Longville the line closed completely, remaining open for freight northwards to Wenlock until 1963.

The branch lost its passenger service in early 1951; five years earlier, Minsterley was busy, with LNW Coal Tank 7740 on a Shrewsbury train at the platform and Coal Engine 28204 on a freight in the sidings. W.A. CAMWELL/STEPHENSON LOCOMOTIVE SOCIETY

The station buildings at Longville remain in use as a private house, much modified but recognizably of railway origin.

Coalport

The Coalport branch closed to passengers on 31 May 1952; it remained open for freight, with several trains daily serving the Lilleshall Company's sidings at Priors Lee. A daily pick-up freight served the full length of the branch until 5 December 1960, when it was cut back to Stirchley. In the meantime, the Lilleshall Company's last blast furnace at Priors Lee had been blown out in 1959 and its railway system had closed. The inevitable final closure of the branch followed on 6 July 1964.

North of Telford Town Park, virtually nothing remains of the route, but southwards to Coalport, it forms part of the Silkin Way footpath (Lewis Silkin was the MP who, in the 1945 Labour administration, piloted the New Towns Act of that year). Nearing Blists Hill, the path passes the former Madeley Market station, still in use as office accommodation by Social Services and still recognizably a railway station. The short tunnel (one of very few in the county) beside the Blists Hill Museum site seems far too low to accommodate a train. The truth is

On 12 September 1959, the SLS 'West Midlands Rail Tour' visited Coalport. Like the steam-hauled special of 1955, it also visited Longville and Minsterley and may well have been their last passenger train. IRONBRIDGE GORGE MUSEUM TRUST

The last train passed through Pipe Gate station, on the North Staffs line to Market Drayton, in 1966, five years before this photograph was taken. Note that the platform is beyond and separate from the station buildings. SHROPSHIRE RAILWAY SOCIETY

that the pathway has been raised: sewer pipes have been laid on the trackbed – an ignominious end to this archetypal LNWR branch line.

Market Drayton to Stoke

That tiny incursion of the North Staffs, into the north-east of the county, ended a few years later when passenger services, two trains daily from Stoke to Market Drayton, were cut back to Silverdale on 7 May 1956. Freight lasted almost ten years longer, ending on 14 February 1966 between Madeley Chord and Market Drayton.

Whitchurch to Chester

Closure to passengers of the former Whitchurch and Tattenhall Railway, on 16 September 1957, deprived Whitchurch of five trains per day to Chester. Freight services lasted until 4 November 1963.

Woofferton to Tenbury Wells

The last Shropshire closure of the pre-Beeching era affected the southern border line from Woofferton to Bewdley. The line west of Tenbury served its community for exactly 100 years – it closed from 31 July 1961. The last through train from Woofferton to Bewdley had actually run on the previous Saturday, 29 July.

CENTRE: This auto-train, propelled by ex-GWR 0-4-2T no. 1445, will run down the main line to Woofferton, then up the branch to Tenbury Wells. It will do so for just two more weeks; 15 July 1961. ARCHIVE IMAGES

RIGHT: The two weeks have passed, and it is the last day of the line from Woofferton – 1445 again with an auto-train at Tenbury Wells on 29 July 1961. ARCHIVE IMAGES

The next few closures had already been planned, and in some cases executed, when Dr Beeching published his infamous Report in early 1963; they are shown in black ('All passenger services to be withdrawn') on the map that accompanied the Report. The same map explains 'Services, which were under consideration in August 1962, and which, in some cases, have already been withdrawn, are included in this map.' On that basis, those closures will be considered with the Beeching cuts.

The Modernization Plan and the Beeching Cuts

The costs of running the railways had risen steadily, while revenues had remained at best static. By the mid-1950s, the railways were making losses. The Modernisation Plan of 1955, backed by substantial investment, provided for replacement of steam by diesel and electric power and, with expected rising traffic levels, forecast that the railways would be profitable again from the early 1960s.

Many aspects of the plan were successful. The fleet of diesel multiple units (DMUs) introduced for secondary and local services was clean and 'modern', with many lesser lines seeing some revival of fortunes after their introduction. But some of the early diesel locomotive classes, untried designs from several different manufacturers, were not a success. The plan also acknowledged that further cuts in the network were required, primarily in areas where duplication of lines and services, a throwback to the days of competing companies, was neither necessary nor economic.

The financial expectations of the plan were not achieved. Losses grew until the British Transport Commission (BTC) could no longer pay the interest on the resulting accumulated loans. Something had to be done. In June 1961, Dr Richard Beeching became chairman of the British Railways Board – a new body created in anticipation of the dissolution of the British Transport Commission. A controversial appointment (his salary, the same as in his previous role at ICI, would be substantially greater

than that of the Prime Minister), his brief was to make the railways pay.

The first Beeching Plan, *The Reshaping of British Railways*, was published in March 1963. The so-called 'axe' was aimed at the least remunerative third of the network, lines that carried just 1 per cent of traffic. Shropshire's railway network would see further trimming.

A more startling Report, *The Development of the Major Trunk Routes*, followed in 1965, highlighting 3,000 miles (4,800km) of railway which 'should be selected for future development'. None of Shropshire's railways were on the map accompanying this Report; to the west of the county, only the South Wales main line, through Newport and Cardiff to Swansea, was included. Fortunately, the implications of that plan were not carried through.

Beeching in Shropshire

Wellington to Much Wenlock

Buildwas station was a minor railway crossroads, where the Severn Valley line was crossed by the Wellington to Much Wenlock railway. On 21 July 1962, ten years after the former through route to Craven Arms had been truncated at Wenlock, trains had to be strengthened to carry those travelling for 'one last time'. Its annual operating loss of over £12,000 compared with fare revenue of just £4,000. Freight to Much Wenlock, and the remaining freight-only section to Longville, ended on 4 December 1963.

At the northern end, a little under half a mile (800m) of track was removed between Ketley Junction and Ketley Town within months of the last passenger train. Freight continued from Ketley Town southwards to Lightmoor Junction until 6 July 1964; the track was then lifted north of Horsehay. At Horsehay, the works of Adamson Alliance (later Adamson Butterley) specialized in the production of bridges and overhead cranes, heavy steel structures that would often require transport by rail. The connection from the works, through the former goods yard, enabled such movements to take place. The company came to an agreement with BR for the

BR Standard 2-6-2T no. 82006 pulls away from Buildwas station with a train for Much Wenlock. The former Ironbridge 'A' Power Station can be seen beyond the station. IRONBRIDGE GORGE MUSEUM TRUST

line from Horsehay to Lightmoor Junction to be retained. The workings gradually dwindled, the last such taking place in May 1979.

Buildwas station has vanished; in its place are the coal unloading hoppers at Ironbridge Power Station – the former 'B' station, built in the mid-1960s after the Severn Valley line closed. The station building at Much Wenlock, derelict for some years, has been renovated as a private house; the preservation developments based around Horsehay are described later.

Bewdley to Tenbury Wells

When the Woofferton to Tenbury service ended in 1961, the intention had been to close the whole through route. As an acknowledgement of the hardship that closure might bring, an experimental service was provided. Consisting of one return service per day from Tenbury to Kidderminster, it was primarily aimed at meeting the needs of local schoolchildren. It lasted just a year – from 1 August 1962, the Tenbury to Bewdley section lost its passenger service. Freight lasted until the start of 1964,

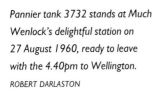

Pannier tank 3732 stands at Much Wenlock's delightful station on 27 August 1960, ready to leave with the 4.40pm to Wellington.
ROBERT DARLASTON

apart from 'as required' trips to Cleobury Mortimer. Servicing the last remaining Admiralty traffic on the former Cleobury Mortimer and Ditton Priors line, they ran until 16 April 1965.

Before closure, the Tenbury line had a glimpse of modernity, when it was used for commissioning new diesel multiple units that were then being built by the Birmingham Railway Carriage and Wagon Company. The sight of these new trains must have been depressingly ironic for local travellers, knowing their own service was doomed.

Ellesmere to Wrexham

Also in 1962, on 10 September the branch line from Ellesmere to Wrexham closed. In 1949, eight trains per day had shuttled back and forth along this former Cambrian Railways byway, taking around thirty-five minutes for the 12¾-mile (20.5km) journey. The line was a haunt of the 'auto-train' – a small (steam) locomotive and a single coach, operated push-pull fashion.

Shrewsbury to Hartlebury Junction

A year later, two more closures affected the county. The Severn Valley line, from Shrewsbury to Hartlebury Junction, had already been scheduled for closure when the Beeching Report was published. Between Bewdley and Shrewsbury, the passenger service was lightly used and for many services a single diesel unit was sufficient for traffic. It closed with effect from 9 September 1963. The southern part of the line is of course now much better known as the Severn Valley Railway. The line south from Bridgnorth carries far more passengers than it ever did – a single carriage would not be sufficient today.

The track was left in place between Buildwas and Shrewsbury to allow delivery of certain very large and heavy items for the construction of Ironbridge Power Station; during that period the Shrewsbury end was also used for testing Sentinel diesel locomotives. It was lifted after deliveries to the power station were complete.

Ex-GWR 0-4-2T no. 1423 stands at Ellesmere station with an Ellesmere to Wrexham Central train, 20 September 1958. Four years later, the Wrexham line closed. G.E.S. PARKER COLLECTION/KIDDERMINSTER RAILWAY MUSEUM

Wellington to Nantwich

The closures listed above were all 'thin lines' – minor single-track railways with sparse traffic – on early BR passenger network maps. The Wellington to Nantwich line, which closed on the same day as the Severn Valley, was a more substantial railway – a bold red line on the map. Double track throughout, five weekday passenger trains ran in each direction between Wellington and Crewe, with two more trains running between Wellington and Market Drayton. During the last year of the line's life, the *Pines Express*, which famously ran from Manchester to Bournemouth, travelled (non-stop) along the line. Its diversion away from the former Somerset and Dorset route between Bournemouth

6813 Eastbury Grange *has run south over the Market Drayton line and will soon join the main line at Wellington. The passenger service ended the previous year, but freight lasted until 1967. Admaston's autumn tints of 2 October 1964 provide a leafy backdrop.*
BERWYN STEVENS

and Bath necessitated route changes further north. It would suffer more changes of route before its last run in 1967.

The Market Drayton line had been an important through route for freight – at one time, as many as twenty freights would traverse the line each day. Many would have run via the former GWR's Wombourne line, which closed in 1965. The proposed marshalling yard at Walcot (*see* below) might have lengthened the line's life, but it was not built and final closure to freight came in 1967.

Wellington to Stafford

The penultimate major closure to have an impact on the county's network affected one of its oldest lines, the passenger service of which had dwindled in latter years. Wellington had been a significant junction on the GWR main line, where passengers could change for services to Coalport, Craven Arms, Nantwich and Stafford. When passenger services to Stafford ended on 7 September 1964, Wellington ceased to be a passenger junction.

Freight lingered on, ending north of Newport two years later; by 1969, Donnington was the line's northern terminus. Coal trains from Granville Colliery continued for another ten years and trains for the Ministry of Defence depot lasted until 1991; the line was then closed and lifted. In the early years of the twenty-first century, track was relaid between Wellington and Donnington, restoring the rail freight service for the MoD and serving a new freight terminal at Hortonwood.

The crew of 46114 Coldstream Guardsman must have had an easy job on this Stafford train at Newport, on 20 December 1960.
HUGH BALLANTYNE/RAILPHOTOPRINTS.CO.UK

Buttington Junction to Whitchurch

Part of a former main line, from Aberystwyth to Whitchurch, this closed in 1965. The through Manchester services had been taken off the line in 1960 and most trains started from or terminated at Whitchurch. In 1963, responsibility for the line passed from the Western Region to the London Midland. Two years later, on 18 January 1965, the railway between Buttington Junction and Whitchurch closed, along with the Llanfyllin branch, which was served from Oswestry.

The former Cambrian Railways network was once well connected. As well as at Oswestry, Whitchurch and Wrexham, it joined to other lines at Aberystwyth, Dolgellau and Afon Wen on the coast, at Builth Road and Three Cocks Junction in the south, and at Buttington. Only the last-named remains – a journey on to today's 'Cambrian' must begin with the former Shrewsbury and Welshpool Railway.

Oswestry to Gobowen

Oswestry's first connection to the national network was its last and was Shropshire's last passenger railway closure. The shuttle service on the county's oldest branch line, between Oswestry and Gobowen, ended on 7 November 1966. Freight trains continued to use this section to gain access to the quarries around Llanyblodwell for another twenty-two years.

Dr Beeching had listed the Central Wales line, the former LNWR/LMS route from Craven Arms to South Wales, for closure. It did not close, although the route into Swansea has changed somewhat. Swansea Victoria station closed in summer 1964 and for a time, diesel trains from Shrewsbury ran to Llanelli. Since the 1970s, they have sensibly reversed there to complete their journey to Swansea (High Street) along the former GWR main line. It is probably significant that at the time of the Beeching cuts, several of the parliamentary constituencies through which the line passed were considered to be marginal. The locomotive-hauled trains are long gone – the line has operated under a Light Railway Order since 1972 as a cost-cutting measure and services have been in the hands of diesel units ever since. The line is, however, maintained to a sufficient standard to carry heavier trains, in the form of occasional steam-hauled specials, or freight diversions.

An unlikely visitor to Oswestry – former Great Central 4-4-2T no. 67442 (LNER/BR class C14) stands with a GWR auto-trailer in the bay platform at Oswestry. The former GWR station is seen to the right and the Crosville bus depot is behind the auto-trailer; 11 May 1949. P.M. ALEXANDER

Reversing the Cuts?

Nationally, there were relatively few closures after Beeching and more recently some lines have reopened to passenger traffic, such as the Cannock Chase line, which for a number of years had been freight only. In Scotland, some lifted lines have been, or are being, relaid and reopened. Could any of Shropshire's closed lines be viable today? There have been frequent suggestions in recent years that the former Shropshire Union line to Stafford, perhaps the ideal route for a reinstated London service, should be reopened. The Campaign for Better Transport's 'Lines that should reopen – Top 36' lists it as a 'missing link that would make the network work better', and also includes Madeley Junction to Madeley 'to connect big/growing places that are not on the rail network'. At the very least, it is interesting to speculate upon such possibilities.

Station Closures

Today, Shropshire's railways radiate from Shrewsbury – towards Chester, Crewe, Wolverhampton, Hereford and Welshpool, with the Central Wales line to Swansea heading for the hills from Craven Arms.

The Beeching era is associated with line closures; we should remember that many passenger-carrying lines felt the 'axe' in a different way. Some of the Beeching Report map's red lines ('services to be retained') were dashed. On such lines, 'All stopping passenger services' were to be withdrawn. Three such lines radiated from Crewe – the west coast main line northwards to Glasgow, the Holyhead line and the North and West as far as Craven Arms. One other Shropshire route – Shrewsbury to Wellington – was affected. Ultimately, however, very few stations in Shropshire were affected in this manner – those stations which closed, on the lines remaining open, mostly closed before Beeching.

Shrewsbury to Chester

There were, for a relatively short period, no fewer than seven stations and halts between Shrewsbury and Gobowen and two more between the latter and Chirk, just across the Welsh border. Trehowell Halt closed in 1951; Leaton, Oldwoods Halt, Baschurch, Stanwardine Halt, Haughton Halt, Rednal and West Felton, Whittington Low Level and Weston Rhyn all lost their passenger services in 1960. Gobowen remains open and there is currently a campaign to reopen the station at Baschurch, not quite halfway from Shrewsbury to Gobowen.

Shrewsbury to Crewe

Despite Beeching's proposal, stopping trains continue to serve the line, a result of strenuous local effort. Hadnall closed before Beeching, in 1960.

Shrewsbury to Wolverhampton

Admaston, Walcot and Upton Magna, on the joint line, had been served by both LMS and GWR before nationalization. By the 1960s, the service was primarily provided by trains running from and to the Wellington to Stafford line – they were closed on the same day as that route closed, 7 September 1964. East of Wellington, the local stations (apart from New Hadley) remain open.

Shrewsbury to Hereford

There were numerous small stations and halts on the line. Within the county, Ashford Bowdler had closed in 1855; all the others apart from Woofferton closed in June 1958. These included Condover, Dorrington, Leebotwood, All Stretton Halt, Little Stretton Halt, Marshbrook, Wistanstow Halt, Onibury and Bromfield. Woofferton closed when the Tenbury Wells line closed on 31 July 1961. Church Stretton, Craven Arms and Ludlow remain open.

Shrewsbury to Welshpool

The intermediate stations at Hanwood, Yockleton, Westbury, Plas-y-Court (halt), Breidden and Buttington all closed in 1960. Only the first four were in Shropshire.

Craven Arms to Swansea

All the Central Wales line stations in Shropshire – Broome, Hopton Heath, Bucknell and Knighton – remain open.

Under Shrewsbury's overall roof: in the bay, 42305 waits with a Swansea Victoria train, while 5033 Broughton Castle is on a Wolverhampton local. Platform 3's 'dog-leg' can be seen to the left. RUSSELL MULFORD

Shrewsbury Station

This underwent major change during the 1960s, perhaps inevitably given the reduction in services. Removal of the overall roof and footbridge at the south end of the station in 1962–3 enabled the reduction in width of the southern end of platform 3. As a result, the dog-leg part way along the platform was eliminated and a through road provided between platforms 3 and 4 for northbound freight. The former central signal box was also taken out of use, no longer needed when most trains were multiple units.

Bay platforms 1 and 2 were no longer required after the Severn Valley line had closed, so were taken out of passenger use, as was platform 3, although it remained available. All of Shrewsbury's passenger trains could be served from the island platform – the subway became the station entrance, in effect, with the booking offices and barriers relocated on to the platform at the top of the subway steps. In the late 1960s, the main station building was threatened with demolition. BR administrative offices had moved to a new building in Chester Street, resulting in the empty building beginning to deteriorate. Happily, it received listed status in 1969 and more recently has been refurbished and brought back into railway use.

Shrewsbury's platform 1 was no longer needed for the Severn Valley trains; instead, it was a convenient place for these coaches from the Vale of Rheidol railway to undergo maintenance in 1971. SHROPSHIRE RAILWAY SOCIETY

Freight in the 1950s

Shropshire's railways still carry a substantial volume of freight, though trains and traffic flows are very different from those of steam days. 'Marshalling Instructions for Through and Important Local Freight Trains', a Western Region document dating from 1958, paints a picture of a vanished era. Little remains today of Shrewsbury's freight yards; the remaining fragments having very different purposes.

In 1958, however, the county's freight yards were hives of activity. Harlescott Sidings took traffic mostly from South Wales, sorting it for various northern destinations, while Coleham yard performed a similar function in the opposite direction. Abbey Foregate's function was more local, dealing with trains heading for medium-range destinations such as Burton-on-Trent and more locally to Donnington, Dawley and Stirchley. Coton Hill dealt with traffic running up and down the former GWR main line and the Severn Valley line.

The site of Coleham yard remains in use by Network Rail, as a permanent way depot and home of a maintenance depot for the locomotives used as part of the Cambrian lines' signalling project. In 1958, the small yard bustled throughout all twenty-four hours of the day. If we take a look at a weekday morning's departures, we may get a flavour of that activity:

- At 12.40am and 1.30am, Mondays only, 8F 2-8-0s were booked to head south for the Central Wales line. Their final destination was Swansea; they would deliver and pick up traffic en route, at Llandovery, Pontardulais and Gorseinon. On days other than Monday, a 1.05am departure, rostered for an ex-GWR 'Grange', would head for Pontypool Road, calling at Hereford and Little Mill Junction.
- At 4.30am, an ex-LMS 0-8-0 would head for Welshpool.
- Another Swansea freight (another 8F) would leave at 5.55am, calling at Craven Arms, Knighton, Llandrindod Wells, Builth Road, Llandovery, Llandilo, Pontardulais and Gorseinon.
- 6.45am saw a Cardiff-bound freight head south behind a 2-8-0 (an LMS 8F on Mondays and Thursdays, a GWR 28XX on other days). Its first stop would be Marshbrook, to detach livestock vehicles.
- A local pick-up freight for Welshpool (ex-LMS 0-8-0) was scheduled to leave at 8.35am, calling to shunt at all stations apart from Hanwood and Buttington.
- Another 8F-hauled Swansea train followed at 9.05am.
- A train for Pontypool Road (8F) left at 10.25am.
- Seven more freights would pull out of the south end of the yard during the afternoon and evening; obviously, the early hours would see fewer passenger trains getting in the way of freight (or vice versa).

BR Standard 4-6-0 no. 75060 pulls away from the exchange sidings at Weston Rhyn with a train of coal from Ifton Colliery to Saltney; 3 March 1967. BERWYN STEVENS

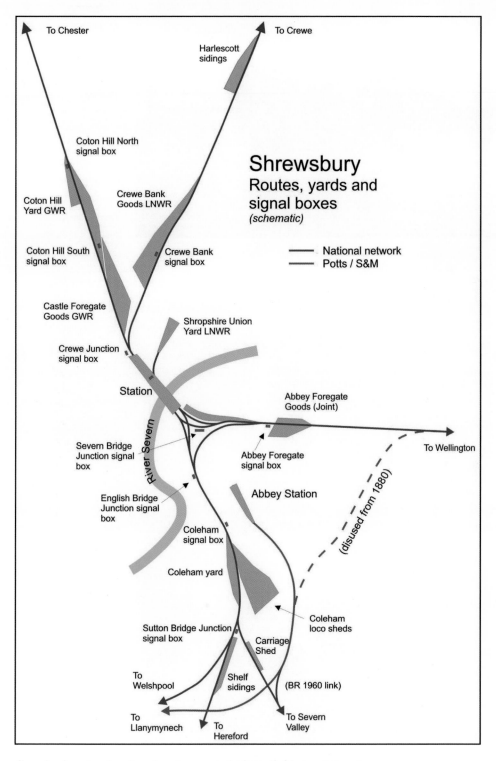

To Chester

To Crewe

Harlescott
sidings

Coton Hill North
signal box

Shrewsbury
Routes, yards and
signal boxes
(schematic)

Crewe Bank
Goods LNWR

Coton Hill
Yard GWR

——— National network
——— Potts / S&M

Coton Hill South
signal box

Crewe Bank
signal box

Castle Foregate
Goods GWR

Shropshire Union
Yard LNWR

Crewe Junction
signal box

Station

Abbey Foregate
Goods (Joint)

River Severn

Severn Bridge
Junction signal
box

Abbey Foregate
signal box

To Wellington

English Bridge
Junction signal
box

Abbey Station

(disused from 1880)

Coleham
signal box

Coleham yard

Coleham
loco sheds

Sutton Bridge Junction
signal box

Carriage
Shed

To
Welshpool

Shelf
sidings

(BR 1960 link)

To
Llanymynech

To
Hereford

To Severn
Valley

Shrewsbury's scattered goods yards as they were in the first half of the twentieth century.

LMS Patriot no. 45530 Sir Frank Ree was rebuilt in 1946 and is seen going well near Whitchurch on 20 August 1964. It was withdrawn from service the following year. BERWYN STEVENS

BELOW: 6976 Graythwaite Hall approaches Shrewsbury with the Dorrington–Kensington milk train in the late 1950s. RUSSELL MULFORD

Shrewsbury and Hereford: ex-LNWR 0-8-0 no. 49341 is at the start of its long slog to Church Stretton as it leans to the curve near Bayston Hill in 1953. RUSSELL MULFORD

On the last weekend of steam at Shrewsbury, an ex-LMS 8F 2-8-0 pulls away from Coton Hill north with a tank train. The extensive yards are evident; Shrewsbury gaol stands out on the skyline; 4 March 1967.
BERWYN STEVENS

All of these trains would be 'fed' by inward movements. For example, at Coton Hill, no fewer than twelve trains were due each working day – in no particular order, three from Swansea, two from Hereford and one each from Craven Arms, Pontypool Road, Welshpool, Minsterley, Hookagate, Hollinswood and Hartlebury. The other yards would be fed in similar fashion; it requires little imagination to see how busy Shrewsbury was in the years before the motorways.

There were, of course, significant freight yards elsewhere in the county, mostly for local traffic – several are mentioned above. The great majority would disappear over the years, the valuable land they occupied today the site of modern supermarkets or housing developments.

Walcot Yard

The 1955 Modernisation Plan proposed the development of new marshalling yards, at various points around the country. One of these could have made major changes to the busy scenes outlined above. An article in the February 1961 *Railway Magazine* describes the Western Region's proposed new Shrewsbury yard, to be constructed at Walcot, between Shrewsbury and Wellington. The down main line would have been diverted some distance southwards and the yard constructed between the

A busy scene at Sutton Bridge Junction in 1953. The signalman takes the Severn Valley line token from the pannier tank's crew; Coleham yard is busy with a train ready to head south and an ex-GWR 0-6-2T stands on the main line with a freight, waiting for the road south.
RUSSELL MULFORD

OFF THE RAILS: BASCHURCH, 1961

A freight for Saltney (Chester) had left Shrewsbury Coton Hill a little before 7.00pm on 13 February 1961. It was stopped at Baschurch at 7.24pm, to set back into the refuge siding and allow a passenger train to pass. The latter left Shrewsbury at 7.09pm. The freight did not manage to reverse fully into the siding, but the signalman assumed that it had done so and, despite a lack of confirmation, cleared his signals. The approaching passenger train then put on steam. The freight driver, seeing the signals cleared ahead of him, assumed a change of plan and began to move forwards, then saw the oncoming passenger train, shut off steam, braked and leapt from the engine, as did the fireman. The passenger engine struck the leading vehicle of the freight and the locomotive's tender, then overturned to come to rest on the opposite line, between the station platforms. A stores van, which had been attached between the locomotive and the passenger carriages, caught fire and burnt out beneath the leading coach, which was also seriously damaged. The driver and fireman of the passenger train, as well as one of two storemen travelling in the stores van, were killed. The other storeman was seriously injured. Two of the twenty-two passengers were slightly injured, as were the freight locomotive crew and the guards of the two trains.

Colonel McMullen concluded in his report that the primary cause of the accident was the signalman's error, although the freight guard appeared to have applied his brake well before the end of the refuge siding, causing the reversing movement to be interrupted. He also commented on the lack of track circuits on the down line, with which the signalman would have known the freight was still fouling the main line.

COTON HILL (SHREWSBURY), 1965

The last few miles of the line from Chester are on a falling gradient, the steepest part of which is the 1 in 100 of Hencote bank. At the foot of the bank Coton Hill North signal box marked the entrance, for freight trains, into Coton Hill yard. Shortly before 6.00am, on 11 January 1965, a Saltney to Pontypool Road freight approached Shrewsbury, hauled by a locomotive that was less than a year old, Brush type 4 (later Class 47) no. D1734.

At the top of Hencote bank, there was a stop sign. Freight trains such as this were required to draw to a stand before continuing down the bank, but the train in question ran straight down the bank without stopping. It entered the Coton Hill goods loop at speed, derailed on trap points at the end of the loop, then ran on for another 70yd (64m) before demolishing the Coton Hill South signal box. The signalman was killed, the driver seriously injured and the locomotive, beyond economic repair, was written off. It was the first of the class to be scrapped; they were in fact still under construction, the last one (D1111) entering service more than two years later.

passenger lines. Consisting of forty-eight hump-shunted marshalling sidings, plus associated reception and departure sidings, the yard would have contained around 38 miles (61km) of track. A subsidiary yard would enable secondary sorting of traffic from the main yard and would also service express freights. Wagon and diesel repair and road–rail trans-shipment facilities would have completed the installation. East of the yard, a new spur would connect to the Wellington–Market Drayton line, so that freight travelling via Crewe could avoid Shrewsbury station altogether by means of the Abbey Curve. Spoil excavated at Walcot was to have provided the required infill for a similar yard proposed for Gloucester.

The justification for this major investment lay in a number of factors. There were numerous yards in the northern part of the Western Region, at Shrewsbury, Wolverhampton, Wrexham and Chester, but none was big enough for the whole area, so much staging from yard to yard and marshalling had to take place. Similar staging through yards was required for the substantial freight flows to and from the London Midland Region. The economic and schedule benefits of through freights were becoming clear – yards such as Walcot would enable the gathering together of traffic to form trains which could then run long distances without remarshalling.

There was much local opposition to the use of the green field site. The local MP, in the debate on the Queen's Speech in October 1959, described it as a 'very nasty incident likely to occur to damage the fair fields of Shropshire'. Ultimately, the plans came to nothing. Regional boundaries changed in 1963 and the Beeching Report was published. Despite the 130 scheduled freight trains passing through Shrewsbury each day in 1963, BR's freight future lay in train-load traffic that did not need marshalling yards. A modernized and electrified Basford Hall yard at Crewe opened in 1961 and Bescot (Walsall) yard was reconstructed, opening in 1966. Bescot, operated today by D.B. Schenker Rail (UK), remains the main freight yard for the West Midlands, though its hump-shunting facility is long gone, as is the wagon-load freight that it was designed for. Basford Hall now serves as a container train hub. It is hard to imagine that there would be any place today for Walcot.

Howard Street Warehouse

At the other end of the scale from Walcot was the Shropshire Union yard in Shrewsbury. The yard, tucked in between the jail and Castle Foregate, was where the Shrewsbury Canal terminated. The LNWR had run lines into the area through a short curved tunnel on the north-east side of Shrewsbury station, midway along its length. During a period of perhaps thirty years from 1859, the canal basin was truncated and the canal arm into the warehouse was filled in, replaced by railway tracks.

The canal basin closed in 1922, though the yard continued to handle rail-borne goods such as bananas, fertilizer, coal and oil until it finally closed in April 1971. As well as a substantial goods shed, there was a fine canal-age warehouse with a frontage on Howard Street. The date over its door proclaims its opening in 1836, initially as a wholesale market for dairy produce. Derelict for a number of years, the grade II listed building has been renovated and now functions as the Buttermarket 'entertainment venue'.

Locomotive Sheds

Whitchurch

Whitchurch locomotive shed, on the LMS route from Shrewsbury and at the north-eastern tip of the former Cambrian, was a subshed of Crewe North, which had the code 5A. Dating from 1883 (a four-road replacement of an 1872 single-road shed), it closed with the Chester passenger service in 1957. All the other sheds (there were not many) in the county were at first allocated Western Region codes.

Shrewsbury

In the earliest days, the four original companies had their own 'engine houses' – but not their main works – in Shrewsbury. The Chester, Hereford and Birmingham companies had their main facilities at the other ends of their lines – the shed and works at Stafford Road, Wolverhampton, would both become major GWR facilities. The Stafford line was, from its opening, part of the much larger LNWR and had no need of separate works facilities. The Shrewsbury and Chester's shed was on a cramped site west of its main line, opposite Castle Foregate goods depot, while the Shrewsbury and Birmingham and the Shropshire Union had sheds either side of the line at Abbey Foregate. The Shrewsbury and Hereford built a shed in the Coleham district, east of the main line, and in a change of heart relocated its works there in 1855. When the Hereford line became part of the joint network, the LNWR moved in. The GWR used Coleham too, though for a while its main shed would be the former S&C shed, and it later built a new shed on the other side of the line in what later became Coton Hill (North) yard. By the end of the nineteenth century, matters had been rationalized – the Abbey Foregate sheds had gone, as had the Coton Hill shed. An expanded Coleham would serve local railways until the end of steam.

That shed was unusual in that it was effectively two sheds in one. The LNWR added a ten-road straight shed in 1877, while in 1883 the GWR built another shed behind the original building, with a turntable in the middle and machinery for locomotive maintenance and repair. Another straight shed was added by the GWR in 1932, in the place of the former wagon repair shed. Ironically, the easternmost side was the Western shed, with the LMS to the west, closest to the running lines.

Before nationalization, the GWR's Shrewsbury locomotives had borne the code 'SALOP', or just 'SLP', while LMS locomotives had carried that company's code '4A'. From 1949, all would carry '84G'. Shrewsbury had been in the Wolverhampton Division of the GWR, which extended from Banbury to Birkenhead. Wolverhampton's Stafford Road and Oxley sheds became 84A and 84B respectively; clearly, Shrewsbury was a little further down the pecking order. Subsheds of 84G were at Clee Hill (closed 14 November 1960),

An interesting line-up at Shrewsbury shed – 'Britannia' no. 70020 Mercury stands beside 2-8-0 3031 and 2-6-0 6337. 3031 is one of the Great Central-designed locomotives built for World War I service. Of 100 bought by the GWR after the war, forty-six entered BR service, 3031 lasting until May 1956. RUSSELL MULFORD

Coalport (closed 31 May 1952, when the passenger service ended), Craven Arms (closed 27 May 1964), Knighton and Ludlow.

In 1950, 120 locomotives were allocated to Shrewsbury: fifty-two of GWR origin; sixty-one of LMS origin; and seven ex-War Department 'Austerity' 2–8–0s. Amongst the GWR contingent were five Star Class 4-cylinder 4–6–0s, much-loved precursors of the Castles, of which eight were resident, including no. 5064 *Bishop's Castle*. The GWR may not have wanted its railway, but it was happy to adopt its name for a top-link locomotive.

The former LMS locomotives included nineteen Black Five 4–6–0s and ten 8F 2–8–0s, plus a goodly number of pre-grouping machines. The five ex-LNWR 0–8–0s are perhaps not unexpected, but there were also four ex-Lancashire and Yorkshire 0–6–0s, of an Aspinall design dating from 1889, plus six former Midland Railway 2F 0–6–0s. The smallest locomotives allocated were Sentinel no. 47183 and former Caledonian Railway 0–4–0ST no. 56027. The Sentinel was the resident Clee Hill shunter and the Caley Pug had been tried there.

Nine years later, in 1959, there were still 105 steam locomotives at Shrewsbury. Significant changes were evident: the Stars had gone and there were only four Castles, but there were now fifteen Halls and notably seven County Class 4–6–0s, including no. 1026 *County of Salop*.

Other newcomers included a pair of Manor 4–6–0s. On the LMS side, all of the pre-grouping types had gone, save one solitary ex-LNWR 0–8–0. There were only nine Black Fives, replaced perhaps by twelve BR Standard Class 5 4–6–0s and there were now seventeen 8Fs.

On 10 September 1960, a regional reorganization gave Shrewsbury Oswestry's 89A code, but from September 1963, the shed was in London Midland Region hands – in future, its locomotives would carry 6D. By 1965, as the end of steam approached, numbers were down to just forty. Newcomers included more Manors – there were now seven on the books – Ivatt 2–6–2Ts and 2–6–0s (three of each), plus some more BR Standard types, four Class 4 4–6–0s and four Class 4 2–6–4Ts. During the year, the Class 4 4–6–0s displaced the Manors from their duties, including the *Cambrian Coast Express*. In March 1967, the shed closed to steam, but continued to function as a locomotive depot until July 1971.

The whole Coleham site has since been cleared and a modern commercial development, Brassey Close, occupies the site. The only former locomotive shed remaining is the first one, the Shrewsbury and Chester's 'engine house', now named Brassey House. It was converted to contain modern apartments as part of the Benbow Quay housing development.

19 September 1965 – almost the end for the Manors at Shrewsbury's Coleham locomotive shed, although 7802 Bradley Manor *survived its subsequent stay in Barry scrapyard and continues to earn its keep on the Severn Valley Railway.* BERWYN STEVENS

It might appear from the above that no named ex-LMS locomotives were allocated to Shrewsbury in the BR period – in fact, six Jubilee 4–6–0s took up residence there in October 1961. Two were there for around a year – the others remained until the Shrewsbury–Wellington–Stafford line closed and the Central Wales line went over to diesel multiple units in 1964.

Similarly, shed allocations do not necessarily reflect the broader picture of locomotives working into the area. The ex-GWR's Kings were permitted to run between Hereford and Shrewsbury in 1951, then from 1961 they were allowed on the Wolverhampton–Chester line. Now in their last days, being displaced elsewhere by diesels, they

began to make more frequent appearances in the county. The Counties were common too – as well as the local engines, Bristol-, Chester- and Wolverhampton-based locomotives would appear. Perhaps two-thirds of the class could regularly be seen at Shrewsbury; in 1959, all of the northern-allocated Counties were at Shrewsbury.

'Foreign' former LMS types would also appear regularly on North and West Expresses between Crewe and Shrewsbury. Patriots, Royal

County of Salop, *no. 1026, stands at Coleham shed. All thirty of the County Class, dating from 1945–7, had gone by the end of 1964.* RailPhotoprints.co.uk COLLECTION

Scots, Jubilees and, latterly, Princess Royal and Coronation Pacifics would arrive and be replaced by a Castle, or, perhaps in earlier years, a Star; heavier trains might be piloted for the climb to Church Stretton. Also regularly seen on the North and West were the BR-built Britannia Pacifics.

Wellington

After Shrewsbury's 84G comes 84H – Wellington was a much smaller shed, with a subshed at Much Wenlock. Its former site, beside the now-disused northern face of the station's island up platform, is now a car park. It seems barely big enough, but in 1950 twenty-four ex-GWR locomotives, 0-6-0 pannier tanks and 2-6-2 tanks were allocated there. Much Wenlock shed was no longer needed when the line to Craven Arms closed in 1951.

By 1959, the total was down to fifteen – eight panniers and seven 2-6-2Ts, of which three were of the relatively new BR Standard Class 3 variety. Passenger trains were still running to Much Wenlock, to Crewe via Market Drayton and to Stafford. Freight lingered on to Coalport. Within five years, most of that traffic had gone and the shed, which had transferred to the London Midland Region with Shrewsbury in 1963, closed in August 1964.

Oswestry

89A Oswestry was the principal shed in the GWR's Central Wales Division (which, of course, had nothing to do with the LNWR/LMS Central Wales line). Other sheds within the division were at Brecon (89B) and Machynlleth (89C), plus there were numerous subsheds. Oswestry's included Llanfyllin and the narrow-gauge shed at Welshpool. The volume of traffic handled on the former Cambrian was relatively small by comparison with the other former GWR divisions – around 120 locomotives were sufficient in 1950. Eleven of the total were at Brecon, the remainder spread equally between Oswestry and Machynlleth.

Most of the fifty-three locomotives allocated to Oswestry in 1950 were relatively small – the three biggest, the Manors, were examples of the GWR's

smallest variety of 4-6-0. Two of them are still with us, 7808 *Cookham Manor* at the GW Society's premises at Didcot, and 7819 *Hinton Manor* on the Severn Valley at Bridgnorth. The latter, built in 1939, was in Shropshire throughout its BR days, starting at Whitchurch and ending at Shrewsbury. At the time of writing it is out of use, on display at its birthplace, Swindon.

Manors aside, Oswestry's stock was interesting and varied. No fewer than eight former Cambrian Railways 0-6-0s were on the books in 1950, as were fourteen Dean Goods 0-6-0s, a GWR class dating back as far as 1883. One of those locomotives, no. 2516, is also preserved at Swindon. One of the last Duke 4-4-0s, no. 9084 *Isle of Jersey*, was there, as were seven of the deceptively modern 'Dukedog' 4-4-0s. In 1950, Oswestry was still providing motive power for the Tanat Valley service. The relatively modern 14XX 0-4-2 tanks, of which Oswestry had seven, were suitable replacements for the elderly 2-4-0 tanks that had operated the line for many years.

Oswestry's stock of locomotives had not dwindled significantly by 1959. Only one 4-4-0 remained, no. 9005, but there were now six Manors – and fifteen modern Ivatt Class 2MT 2-6-0s, an LMS design with a light axle loading, eminently suitable for Cambrian duties.

When Shrewsbury became 89A in 1960, Oswestry was recoded 89D. As with Shrewsbury and Wellington, it became a London Midland shed in 1963 (6E), until that part of the former Cambrian network closed in January 1965. Many of its locomotives were transferred to Shrewsbury.

Craven Arms

Craven Arms was subject to some interesting speculation for a time. The 'strategic reserve' was a mythical secret store of steam locomotives, ready to spring into action should there be an energy crisis. The locomotive shed (a subshed of Shrewsbury) had closed in 1964 and was demolished in the 1970s, but the carriage shed alongside remained, doors locked. It was rumoured that something important was locked inside – a number of modern steam locomotives perhaps? Almost 1,000 steam locomotives had been built to (mostly) new designs by British Railways and, with just a handful of exceptions, had been consigned to the scrapyards. Many had seen under ten years' service. In the event, there were no such locomotives in store at Craven Arms (or elsewhere), though the myth is revived from time to time.

The reality was that, during the Cold War, a number of 'Mobile Control Trains' were formed and some such carriages were stored at Craven Arms. When the decision was taken to dispose of them, a number were bought for preservation. Two ex-GWR coaches from Craven Arms went to the Severn Valley Railway, which also acquired three ex-LNER teak-bodied vehicles from the Eastern Region control trains.

Summer Saturdays, 1966

Shropshire's passenger network has not changed significantly since the Oswestry–Gobowen shuttle ended, although the pattern and intensity of services has altered considerably. 1966 was the last full year of steam and the last full year of the main line to Paddington.

A Shrewsbury departures timetable for summer Saturdays 18 June to 3 September 1966 gives a flavour of the importance that would soon fade. At the height of the summer peak, more than ninety passenger trains were scheduled to depart. In addition to the normal service trains, numerous extras were scheduled, taking holidaymakers to the West Country and the Welsh coast.

The first hour of the day provided a brief calm before the storm. Between 1.00am and 3.00am, no fewer than four trains would call on their way, via Hereford and the Severn Tunnel, to the West Country. Four more would call between 10.00am and 11.00am. Of those eight, four were for Paignton, three for Penzance and one for Plymouth. Only the 2.41am to Penzance included sleeping cars and only the 10.20am for Plymouth offered refreshments – 'full restaurant service', as well as snacks and drinks.

7819 Hinton Manor *climbs past Hookagate with the down* Cambrian Coast Express, *26 September 1964. During the following year, the Manors would be displaced by the BR Standard 75XXX 4-6-0s; two years later steam and the* Cambrian Coast Express *would be gone.*
BERWYN STEVENS

At 11.59am, what appears to be the *Pines Express* (not shown as such on the timetable) would stop, before continuing its journey from Manchester, calling at Wolverhampton, Birmingham Snow Hill, Oxford, Reading West, Basingstoke, Winchester City, Southampton Central, Brockenhurst, Bournemouth Central, Branksome, Parkstone and Poole. Two more trains for the West Country would call in the afternoon, both heading for Plymouth.

The return workings, somewhat less exciting, are also shown. There are sixteen trains travelling via Crewe to Manchester Piccadilly, Liverpool Lime Street, or, by splitting at Crewe, both destinations.

On the Great Western main line, no fewer than ten trains ran to Birkenhead, calling at Gobowen, Ruabon, Wrexham General, Chester General, Hooton and Rock Ferry (change for Liverpool Central Low Level). In the up direction, nine trains ran to Paddington.

The Cambrian holiday traffic must not be forgotten. One of the Paddington trains mentioned above was the up working of the *Cambrian Coast Express*, leaving Shrewsbury at 12.55. The outbound working is not shown on the timetable and the 12.55 carries the warning 'Not Saturdays 16 July to 27 August'. Trains from the GW main line to the Cambrian coast, if they were to stop at Shrewsbury station, would have to reverse, further adding to the potential congestion in the station. Consequently, trains taking the direct route round the Abbey Curve to the Welshpool line would not appear on the station departures board.

Farewell to the Main Line, 4 March 1967

When the last shuttle from Oswestry arrived there in November 1966, Gobowen was still on a main line from London to Merseyside. However, electric trains began running the full length of the former LMS London to Liverpool route in 1966 and the Birmingham area electrification was completed and opened from 6 March 1967. The previous Saturday, 4 March 1967, is a date firmly etched into the memories of Shropshire railway enthusiasts.

To mark the end of the main line, two special trains ran from Paddington to Birkenhead and back, *The Birkenhead Flyer* and *The Zulu*. On the same day, the last *Cambrian Coast Express* ran, steam-hauled to the end.

The Birkenhead Flyer, the 8.25am from Paddington, would follow the original GWR route to Birmingham, via Didcot and Oxford; *The Zulu* would leave Paddington at 8.40am and run along the newer direct line through High Wycombe, thus overtaking *The Birkenhead Flyer*. Diesel-hauled from Paddington, steam took over at Didcot and Banbury respectively, in the shape of 4079 *Pendennis Castle* and 7029 *Clun Castle* (the small south-west Shropshire town never had a railway). They would then both run via Birmingham Snow Hill, Wolverhampton Low Level and Shrewsbury to Chester, where, as ever, the trains reversed and were hauled to Birkenhead by BR Standard 4–6–0s. Both Castles were by then in the hands of preservation. *Pendennis* was only the seventh of the class to be built, in 1924; it saw forty years of service. *Clun* was a youngster, built by BR to the same design in May 1950. It was the last Castle in BR service, withdrawn at the end of 1965.

End of steam: 75033 is turned at Shrewsbury Coleham shed on 4 March 1967, when it had the honour of working the last up Cambrian Coast Express. RUSSELL MULFORD

The specials to mark the end of the former GWR main line as a through route were heavily oversubscribed; as a result, there were reruns the following day. 7029 Clun Castle is heading for Chester on Hencote bank. Coton Hill North signal box is seen behind the train; 5 March 1967.
BERWYN STEVENS

The Chester to Shrewsbury line was by then part of the London Midland Region. Former GWR steam had been displaced and trains were in the hands of ex-LMS Black Fives. Nevertheless, in the last year of the through Paddington service, trains were timed to run the 18 miles (30km) from Gobowen to Shrewsbury in 'even time' – a 'mile-a-minute'. In those dying days of steam, crews were determined to show what obsolete motive power was still capable of. Speeds of over 90mph (145km/h) were recorded and the distance was covered on one occasion in just sixteen minutes and fifteen seconds.

Despite the swansong heroics, it was the two specials that really drew the crowds. The fine spectacle of the two beautifully restored loco-motives hauling their trains through the county marked the end of a once-important route. The long-disused spur from Stafford Road Junction to Wolverhampton High Level was reinstated and trains from Shrewsbury to London Euston would, for the immediate future, run as they did in 1854, along the Stour Valley route to Birmingham New Street. Had circumstances and railway politics been different, that could have been the case many years earlier. In the meantime, most of the GWR line from Wolverhampton to Birmingham, after becoming completely disused and lifted, has been reinstated as a modern tramway.

Preserved 7029 Clun Castle is at Coleham shed, Shrewsbury, on 24 September 1966, and appears to be leaking somewhat. It had worked in with the annual special for Talyllyn Railway members, which had continued to the coast behind a pair of 75XXX 4-6-0s. Shed foreman, Mr Roberts, who retired with steam in March 1967, looks on, wondering whether it will make it back to Banbury with the return working. BERWYN STEVENS

The North and West

Little more than three years later, similar major changes affected the North and West, though without ceremony. From the start of the new time-table in May 1970, trains from the north-west of England to the south-west would no longer run via Shrewsbury, Hereford and the Severn Tunnel. For the foreseeable future, DMUs running between Crewe and Cardiff would form the basis of the service.

Things would eventually improve, with the service reverting to loco-haulage from the mid-1970s and later extending beyond Crewe and Cardiff, but the days of regular services from Manchester and Liverpool to the West Country, via Shrewsbury, Hereford and the Severn Tunnel, were over.

Post-Beeching Railways

The wholesale modernization of motive power with diesel (seen as an interim measure) and electric traction was really beginning to eat into the steam fleets by the time Dr Beeching arrived on the scene. At nationalization, BR acquired perhaps 20,000 steam locomotives (admittedly some were little better than scrap) and built around 2,500 new ones in the years to 1960, of which 1,500 were to pre-nationalization designs. Nevertheless, steam finished nationally in August 1968 – inevitably many locomotives were scrapped that should have

No. 6000 King George V *launched the 'Return to Steam' programme of steam specials in 1972 and was a familiar sight on the North and West with specials in the 1970s and 1980s. It was no stranger to the route – it is seen here twenty years earlier, approaching Shrewsbury from the south in 1952.* RUSSELL MULFORD

The LMS Pacifics were frequently seen at Shrewsbury, particularly in their declining years when they were being displaced by diesels on the main line from London Euston. 46238 City of Carlisle pulls away from the station with a 'North and West Express', which probably arrived behind a former GWR Castle or King. RUSSELL MULFORD

Unrebuilt Patriot no. 45539 E.C. Trench *appears to be going well with a southbound 'stopper' to Hereford in 1954. A pannier tank is at work on the 'Shelf' sidings. RUSSELL MULFORD*

BELOW: The Western Region's diesel-hydraulics were seen regularly in their early days, less so after Shrewsbury's transfer to the London Midland Region. Warship D817 Foxhound *(BR Class 42) is seen arriving with a 'North and West Express'. The locomotives had short lives: D817 entered traffic in March 1960 and was withdrawn eleven years later. RUSSELL MULFORD*

D1000 Western Enterprise, *wearing 'desert sand' livery, was barely six months old when it pulled away from Shrewsbury with a Paddington to Birkenhead train in May 1960. HUGH BALLANTYNE/ RailPhotoprints.co.uk)*

Warship D834 Pathfinder *(BR Class 43) passes under Abbey Foregate signal gantry with a Paddington train. Like D817, it was withdrawn from service in 1971. RUSSELL MULFORD*

been good for another twenty years. By the end of 1970, most of the Beeching closures had been implemented – some 4,000 miles (6,400km) in the years 1963 to 1970, on top of more than 3,000 miles (4,800km) in the years 1950 to 1962. Although a handful of closures took place after 1970, the total mileage affected was small.

Wagon-load freight, especially the archaic loose-coupled unbraked variety, had almost disappeared. Its replacement ran on rubber tyres on Britain's expanding motorway network. Much of the remaining rail-borne freight would be conveyed in modern fully braked trains, such as the 'merry-go-round' (mgr) block coal trains running between colliery and power station, or the Freightliner container train. The 'new' railway of the early 1970s (though much of its infrastructure was still steam-age) was almost immeasurably different from that of the 1950s. The steam-hauled local train, stopping at neat little country stations, with well-tended flower beds (station staff had little else to do, for much of the day) had seemed timeless, but its time had passed. Its replacement, if it ran on rails, was typically a no longer modern diesel unit, stopping at a bare, unstaffed platform with at best a draughty shelter of the kind usually found at a bus stop, or ramshackle redundant buildings. It is perhaps unsurprising that passenger numbers continued their steady decline. Nevertheless, the steam branch-line era remained firmly in memory. Given the existence of many recently closed, and in some cases still reasonably intact branch lines, the heritage railway movement was primed for a strong take-off in the 1960s and 1970s.

Post-Steam Passenger Services

Not only had steam gone – so had Shropshire's main lines. When the North and West through services ended in 1970, the scene for Shropshire's railways was, especially for the railway enthusiast, fairly bleak. The county was, to a degree, in isolation. Most services did not run very far north, east or south. Other than the solitary London Euston train, or a trip to Aberystwyth, most journeys of any length would require at least one change of train.

In the immediate post-steam years, local services were in the hands of the first-generation diesel units, which were not the last word in comfort. Their bogies had a tendency to 'hunt', fumes from the oil-fired heaters would drift into the carriages and vibration from the under-floor engines had a tendency to shake and rattle the interior fittings of the coaches (and their passengers …). The informed traveller would choose seats in the unpowered centre cars of three-car units.

The early 1970s were undoubtedly a low point for the county's rail services, but by the mid-1980s, revival was in the air. A study below of timetables from the period – London Midland, May 1968 to May 1969, and BR all-line, May 1985 to May 1986 – gives a flavour of those times.

Western Region Hymek diesel-hydraulic D7026 stands outside Shrewsbury's overall roof on 14 June 1962. Judging by the gaps in the roof, and what looks suspiciously like a contractor's gas bottle in the left foreground, removal work has begun. R.A. WHITFIELD/ *RailPhotoprints.co.uk*

SHROPSHIRE RAILWAYMEN – ROB WESTON

Rob was a signalman for BR from the late 1970s into the early 1980s, working in several boxes, mainly Dorrington, on the Hereford line, and Allscott, beside the sugar factory on the Wolverhampton line. He also worked, on occasion, at Harlescott Crossing ('a noisy box'), Crewe Bank ('dirty – dust from the coal terminal'), Wem, Prees, Leaton, Baschurch, Gobowen North and Coton Hill North. His training was in Shropshire boxes too – Whitchurch and Gobowen South.

By the late 1970s, Dorrington was, and still is, the first box south of Shrewsbury and was quite busy when Rob was there. Stone was still being worked from Bayston Hill Quarry, where the siding connected to the main line by a south-facing point. Whichever direction a train might be heading, it had to be taken at least as far south as Dorrington, the first place where it could reverse. There might typically be three stone trains per day, occasionally more, usually with a Class 40 diesel at the head. There were also, of course, the local passenger services to Cardiff and Swansea, plus parcels and mail (the Crewe–Cardiff TPO) and other freight up and down the North and West. Rob remembers a 'two till ten' shift (14:00–22:00) when no fewer than forty-one train movements were logged. Dorrington was once known for its milk traffic and though this had ended, the remaining sidings might see use for permanent way traffic.

Dorrington box was, like many on the network, a quiet spot, some distance from the nearest road. Allscott, by then the only signal box between Shrewsbury (Abbey Foregate) and Wellington, was perhaps even quieter. Rob enjoyed the work and the environment – the job was 'doable', a position of responsibility without pressure or stress and the quiet was the pleasant quiet of the countryside.

Allscott box was on the opposite side of the railway from the sugar factory, with no road access – Rob parked in the factory car park and walked through the works to start his shift. The box controlled loops either side of the main line where freight could 'go inside' to allow faster trains to pass and controlled traffic in and out of the sugar factory. Lacking mains, water had to be carried in from the factory labs.

Rob started at Allscott in 1978 just as the season's sugar beet 'campaign' had begun. By this time, beet arrived by road, but coal and limestone still came in by rail. In 1978 (the last year it happened), excess beet was taken away by rail, usually to the Colwick factory in Nottinghamshire. Rob has less than happy memories of these workings. Trains were scheduled to leave the exchange sidings a little after 10.00pm, with Rob 'switching out' the box at 11pm and heading for home. But train crews knew about the handy hostelry nearby, where they could pass the time before their scheduled departure. Inevitably, the train was late leaving and Rob would be stuck in the box, unable to switch out until it had gone. BR eventually agreed to an hour's overtime to cover the possibility of a late departure of the sugar-beet train – a 'sweetener' perhaps?

Rail-borne deliveries of coal and limestone ended during the next few years. The traffic was served by local freight trains running between Bescot and Coton Hill, but BR wanted block trains, not wagon-loads, and the rolling stock and handling facilities were life-expired. By summer 1982, the limestone traffic had ended, but coal was still coming in by rail as the factory stocked up for the autumn campaign. Much coal had arrived in June – Rob remembers the factory traffic foreman commenting how they had 'never had it this good', but the following month coal was arriving by road. One day in July, a pair of Class 20 diesels arrived, with a brake van, and left with the remaining empty coal wagons. Rail traffic at Allscott had ended.

Rob's days at Allscott also ended that year when the two-shift operation of the box was reduced to a single daytime shift; a few years later the signal box closed. There was no longer a night train to Colwick to deal with.

Allscott Sugar Wks signal box, beside the Shrewsbury to Wellington line, as seen in 1971. SHROPSHIRE RAILWAY SOCIETY

Class 20 diesels power a train of coal empties from Ironbridge Power Station past Cherry Tree Hill, at the head of Coalbrookdale, in August 1987.

Class 24 no. 5080 is about to bring its stone train off the Cambrian's Porthywaen branch to join the route of the former main line at Llynclys Junction; March 1973. RailPhotoprints.co.uk COLLECTION

A plain diet of DMUs was on offer at Shrewsbury in the early 1970s. A Class 120 DMU for Llanelly via the Central Wales line stands in platform 4, May 1970, during the week after the North and West through expresses ended.

The North and West

In 1968–9, five southbound North and West trains, mostly calling only at Shrewsbury, ran during the daytime: in order, from Liverpool to Plymouth; Manchester to Cardiff; Manchester to Plymouth; then two more from Manchester to Cardiff. Local trains were sparse. Towns such as Ludlow saw just five Shrewsbury to Hereford 'stoppers' calling each weekday, though one of the Manchester to Cardiff trains also stopped there, providing Ludlow with its only longer-distance service. There were also mail trains (usually with passenger accommodation), such as the Liverpool to Cardiff service, departing from Shrewsbury at 2.20am, or the York to Aberystwyth train, calling at Whitchurch before departing from Shrewsbury at 3.15am. The Manchester to Penzance sleeper arrived at Shrewsbury at 2.32am, departing ten minutes later.

North of Shrewsbury things were a little better. Eight Crewe to Shrewsbury locals ran southwards each weekday. The first omitted stops at Prees and Yorton, the remainder served all stations. Some longer-distance trains also served Whitchurch.

By 1985, the long-distance expresses had gone, but some medium-distance services had returned.

A southbound Crewe–Cardiff service hurries past the loop and siding at Woofferton on 2 June 1979.

In addition to local trains between Crewe and Shrewsbury, a number of Crewe to Cardiff and Manchester (or Liverpool) to Cardiff services were operating. Usually locomotive-hauled, short rakes of MkI coaches provided a degree of passenger comfort. In the earliest years, Class 25s predominated, then larger locomotives began to appear. For a time, in the 1980s, trains from Manchester to Cardiff were diagrammed to form a Cardiff to Portsmouth service (and vice versa) and, as a result, the Southern Region Class 33 locomotives became a familiar sight in the Marches. Nevertheless, the 1985–6 timetable shows just seven southbound trains calling at towns such as Ludlow on a weekday. Craven Arms and Church Stretton fared a little better, as they were also served by the Central Wales line trains, which saw five trains in each direction every weekday.

For a time, Southern Region Class 33 diesels were a regular sight on the North and West. Here, 33 056 The Burma Star approaches Craven Arms, at the site of the junction for the Bishop's Castle Railway, Stretford Bridge, on 13 July 1983.

Some long-distance trains still used the North and West in the 1980s – this is the Stirling to Newton Abbot Motorail service, passing through the hills near Church Stretton in October 1984. BERWYN STEVENS

47 538 arrives at Shrewsbury with a Cardiff–Crewe service on a warm summer's evening; 3 July 1986.

Wolverhampton to Chester

When the May 1968–9 timetable took effect, the Paddington trains had gone, but local services on the former GWR main line were still frequent. The Shrewsbury to London Euston train and most of the local trains used Wolverhampton High Level. The locals were either Shrewsbury to Wolverhampton, or Chester to Wolverhampton services. The timetable shows six local trains, four of them starting from Wellington, scheduled to run along the old route to Wolverhampton Low Level, from where there was still a roughly hourly stopping service to Snow Hill; however, use of the old route into Low Level ended in 1968.

Stations along the Wolverhampton line were well served – more than twenty eastbound trains called at Wellington. But most were 'stoppers', taking around 55 minutes for the 30-mile (48km) journey. North of Shrewsbury, passengers intending to travel from Gobowen to Shrewsbury had eleven trains to choose from.

On summer Saturdays, things became a little more interesting, with four trains for the Welsh coast. One from London Euston, two from Birmingham and one from Wolverhampton, these locomotive-hauled trains would reverse at Shrewsbury, to head variously for Aberystwyth, Barmouth and Pwllheli.

In the mid-1980s, there were still eleven trains from Gobowen to Shrewsbury. However, the first of these, the locomotive-hauled 6.25am from Chester, continued to Wellington and then ran non-stop to Wolverhampton. After a change of locomotive, it would head for London Euston. Six more London Euston trains would depart from Shrewsbury, at two-hourly intervals through the day. It was a good service, although there were fewer trains than in 1965, when there were nine weekday services to the capital. But, in 1985, Shrewsbury to London took three hours or slightly less (it would have been even quicker if a locomotive change was not needed at Wolverhampton). Twenty years earlier, the fastest train could match that – the up *Cambrian Coast Express* was scheduled to take three hours and two minutes – but most trains took nearer three and a half hours.

The service to Birmingham was not impressive. It was provided mostly by the London Euston trains, typically taking an hour and nine minutes from Shrewsbury to New Street. Today's hourly fast trains, if they are not scheduled to stop at Smethwick Galton Bridge, are twenty minutes quicker.

The Cambrian

Six weekday trains ran from Shrewsbury to Aberystwyth in 1968–9, one of which started from Wolverhampton, and there was a gap in services of almost four hours during the afternoon. Passengers for Barmouth and Pwllheli had to change at Machynlleth. There was no Sunday service.

The 1985–6 timetable still shows just six weekday Shrewsbury to Aberystwyth trains (plus an extra train on Mondays); there are also two through trains to Pwllheli. Two trains – one for Pwllheli, one for Aberystwyth – started from Crewe. On Saturdays, one train ran from Birmingham to Pwllheli and two from London Euston to Aberystwyth. On Sundays, during the summer peak, a train ran from New Street to Barmouth (arr. 12.13pm), with connections at Dovey Junction for Aberystwyth. Returning from Barmouth at 5pm, it was clearly aimed at the West Midlands day-tripper market.

The Serpell Report

1982 was the low point for passenger traffic on the British Rail network, with a corresponding low in revenue. The Government commissioned Sir David Serpell to examine the state of the railways and to evaluate options for the future. When the Report was published, options included one that would keep 99 per cent of the network's route miles intact, though with closure of some small stations. The headline-grabbing option was for a truly commercial network. All cross-country passenger services would cease. No trains would run north of Edinburgh and Glasgow, or in England west of Bristol. Within Wales, only the capital would retain its rail service. No trains at all would run

The Ironbridge line: the DMU crossing the Albert Edward Bridge is conveying a group from the Institute of Electrical Engineers on a visit to Ironbridge Power Station on 9 June 1979. The chimneys of Ironbridge 'A' are just visible behind the bridge.

west of the Birmingham–Crewe–Liverpool route. Shropshire's railways would disappear entirely.

The Report was published at the end of 1982, but a general election was due the following year. Perhaps unexpectedly, rail use grew significantly in the following years and by the end of the decade, Serpell had been forgotten.

Railway Revival

After the long decline, the last twelve years of British Railways (trading, by now, as British Rail) saw a revival in fortunes and figures have continued to grow since privatization. Modern traction helped to reverse the downward trend – a notable upward movement followed the introduction of the 'Intercity 125' in 1976 – but, by then, much of the network had gone.

During the early 1980s, the main station building at Shrewsbury, disused for a number of years and at one time threatened with demolition, was

ABOVE: *The Ironbridge line: 58 035 has arrived at the power station with a train of coal. Seen in the process of running round, it will soon begin to unload; August 1987.*

The Ironbridge line: passengers to Coalbrookdale. On 27 May 1979, the first train from the temporary platform built to serve the museum heads over the viaduct, crossing one of the pools that provided water power for Darby's furnaces. A service of four trains each Sunday – two from Birmingham and two from Wolverhampton – ran through the summer months, but was not repeated the following year. A similar service was tried in 1988 – again, it operated just the one summer.

Railway revival: the newly reintroduced Cambrian Coast Express *arrives at Telford Central in the early evening of the station's opening day, 12 May 1986.*

refurbished and brought back into use. Railway revival was definitely in the air when Telford Central opened on 12 May 1986. The new town already had stations at Wellington and Oakengates, as well as New Hadley Halt, midway between the two. While Oakengates was only ever a local station, Wellington was – and still is – a substantial main-line station. But Telford's new town centre was in the eastern part of the designated area. Close to the M54 motorway, with what was thought to be ample space for car parking and just a few hundred yards from the shopping centre, the station was intended to be Telford's principal station. It has proved to be hugely successful – serving around a million passengers per year, it is second in numbers only to Shrewsbury. Happily, fears in the western part of Telford for Wellington station were unfounded. The county's third station is used by more than half a million passengers per year.

Telford's gain was New Hadley's loss. Dating from 1934, it was the county's last survivor of the GWR's numerous halts. Little used, the basic wooden structure was in need of repair.

On the same day as Telford Central opened, a revived *Cambrian Coast Express* service was introduced, as an extension of one of the London Euston–Shrewsbury trains. Calling at Telford's new station in the early evening, the down train would arrive in Aberystwyth around 9.00pm; its up counterpart left a little after 7.00am to deliver its passengers to London around midday.

Another aspect of railway revival became apparent from the mid-1980s. Since the end of steam, local passenger services had been operated by the first-generation DMUs, whose basic design dated from the 1950s. In 1985, the second-generation units began to appear, initially in the form of the Class 150 'Sprinters'. With their sliding doors and air suspension, and 285bhp engines in every car, they accelerated smartly and rode smoothly – by comparison with the older units, they really seemed, at the time, to represent a new era of rail travel. In fact, the 150s were the most basic new design to appear (if one discounts the four-wheeled rail buses that appeared around the same time – which, fortunately, were never rostered for use in Shropshire).

The Cambrian Coast Express *has arrived at Shrewsbury and 37 426 Y Lein Fach/Vale of Rheidol has coupled at the rear, ready to haul the train to Aberystwyth; 12 May 1986.*

New trains 1: The Class 150s were the first of the new-generation DMUs to appear on Shropshire's railways. 150 110 has just left Cosford on its way to Shrewsbury; April 1988.

Whilst the 150s were more suitable for commuter services, the better-equipped 155, 156 and 158 units soon began to appear on longer-distance services. The 158s in particular, with their top speed of 90mph (145km/h), raised the standards for rail services in the area. These new trains eventually replaced not only the first-generation multiple units, but also (to the dismay of many railway enthusiasts) the loco-motive-hauled trains on the Crewe–Cardiff route. By the time privatization appeared on the horizon, the so-called 'heritage' DMUs had largely gone from the area.

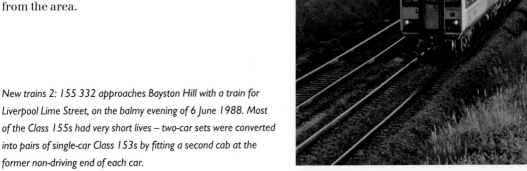

New trains 2: 155 332 approaches Bayston Hill with a train for Liverpool Lime Street, on the balmy evening of 6 June 1988. Most of the Class 155s had very short lives – two-car sets were converted into pairs of single-car Class 153s by fitting a second cab at the former non-driving end of each car.

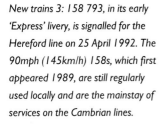

New trains 3: 158 793, in its early 'Express' livery, is signalled for the Hereford line on 25 April 1992. The 90mph (145km/h) 158s, which first appeared 1989, are still regularly used locally and are the mainstay of services on the Cambrian lines.

CHAPTER 5

Minor Lines

The Bishop's Castle Railway

Shropshire's minor lines are remembered with some affection, perhaps none more so than the Bishop's Castle Railway (BCR). Perhaps it is admiration for the underdog – the old-fashioned corner shop struggling to stay in business in the face of competition from the major supermarkets. Its demise would cause a sense of loss, even if we very rarely used it. Such was the case with the Bishop's Castle Railway, notable, or notorious, for operating for no fewer than sixty-nine of its seventy years in the hands of the Official Receiver. Bishop's Castle itself was no stranger to notoriety, having been, until the Reform Act of 1832, one of the numerous 'rotten boroughs' – parliamentary constituencies where the handful of votes needed to elect the

borough's two MPs could easily be bought by local landowners. Even today, the town has a distinct feel of belonging to an earlier age.

The railway's precarious life began in 1860, planned by local businessmen to link the Shrewsbury and Hereford line at Stretford Bridge, near Craven Arms, to the Oswestry and Newtown Railway near Montgomery. From Stretford Bridge the line would follow the scenic Onny valley to Lydham Heath, where a junction would be made with a short branch line to Bishop's Castle. The BCR obtained its Act of Parliament in July 1861. A further Act, dated 29 June 1865, authorized an extension from Chirbury to Minsterley, terminus of a branch line from the Shrewsbury and Welshpool Railway, which would have given Bishop's Castle a moderately direct link to the county town. By this

BCR No. 1, a former GWR 0-4-2T, stands with a passenger train at Bishop's Castle station. A goods guards van is connected between the locomotive and its two 6-wheeled coaches; 30 July 1930. DON POWELL COLLECTION/KIDDERMINSTER RAILWAY MUSEUM

The end is drawing nigh on the BCR: 0-6-0 Carlisle, *built by Kitson of Leeds in 1867, is leaving Bishop's Castle with a mixed train in 1934.* PHOTOGRAPHER UNKNOWN/KIDDERMINSTER RAILWAY MUSEUM

date, construction of the line between Stretford Bridge Junction and Bishop's Castle was nearing completion. The junction at Lydham Heath had been planned as a triangle, so that trains from either direction could run directly to Bishop's Castle – but the direct side of the triangle was never built, nor were any lines on the intended continuation westwards. Every train that ever ran from Craven Arms to Bishop's Castle had to reverse at Lydham Heath.

Construction had commenced in 1863, but the contractor, Thomas Savin, was by then in financial difficulties, becoming bankrupt in 1866. A local contractor, G. M. Morris, continued the construction of the railway from 1864. Although only a single line was ever laid, the formation was constructed to accommodate double track. The magnificent station building at Plowden remains testimony to the unfulfilled expectations of the railway's promoters.

When the line from Stretford Bridge to Bishop's Castle was complete, in October 1865, it was immediately opened, despite the terminus station being incomplete and without Board of Trade approval. When Col. Yolland inspected the line in December, he refused to allow the opening. Further minor improvements were required, which, when implemented, enabled the Bishop's Castle Railway to open officially on 1 February 1866.

Traffic on the new railway was rarely better than light. 1866 was not a good year for railway companies generally. The Bishop's Castle Railway was not alone in being adversely affected by the collapse of the Overend, Gurney Bank, which went into liquidation in June of that year. In the ensuing financial crisis, bank rates rose to 10 per cent for three months. More than 200 companies failed as a result. The plans for expansion beyond Lydham Heath were abandoned and the company was effectively bankrupt by the end of the year.

Happily, the arrival of the bailiffs was not the end of the line. The subsequent sale of assets cleared much of the debt and the biggest purchaser, the Midland Wagon Company, leased the rolling stock back to the company. Along with the debenture holders, it felt that the line had potential. Trains continued to run, although the railway remained in the hands of the receiver.

Clearly the future would not be easy. The receiver seemed to believe that the railway had a greater value as a going concern than if sold off piecemeal, but there were still a number of unhappy investors. On the other hand, some landowners, whose loss was the value of their land used by the railway, viewed it as investment in a valuable community asset. Problems would nevertheless emerge on occasion. One such investor, a Dr Frank Beddoes, was owed £800 for land. After he died in 1887, his widow took the company to court and as a result the bailiffs were called in.

Attempting to force the issue (and payment), the bailiffs had a couple of lengths of rail removed, plus a fence built across the line, near Horderley, a couple of miles from Stretford Bridge. They then sat back beside the track to keep an eye on things. After a week or so, the burghers of Bishop's Castle were getting restless and the LNWR was increasingly concerned about a number of their wagons, which were on the wrong side of the blockade. One evening, a couple of gentlemen happened by the bailiffs in their lonely vigil and, after a while, suggested that they might accompany them for a warm-up and a drink at a local inn. It was most unlikely that anyone would try to run a train at that hour. While the beer flowed, the rails were

The goods shed at Bishop's Castle survived for many years after the railway closed. It is seen here in use by the local sawmill and timber merchant on 25 November 1977. Sadly, it has since been demolished. STEVE PRICE

replaced and an engine gently passed down the line to Craven Arms. The luckless bailiffs only realized what was happening when they heard the locomotive, with its loaded wagons, working hard back up the line. The 1887 closure was not the only one – the line became notorious for them.

In the 1890s and the early years of the twentieth century, the railway made small profits and thoughts were revived of completing the originally planned through route, but nothing came of this. At the grouping of the railways in 1923, it was hoped that the railway might be absorbed into the GWR, but in common with a number of other minor railways across the country, it remained 'outside'.

Things gradually worsened. Closure crises came and went; questions were asked in the House, but with road transport in the ascendancy, the BCR remained bankrupt and unwanted. In 1931, W.H. Austen, assistant to Colonel Stephens (*see* below), paid a visit, but nothing came of it. Physically, the railway had reached a state of utter decrepitude. The line that Colonel Stephens did not want finally closed on 20 April 1935, with dismantling beginning soon after. In February 1937, the last stretch of line was lifted near Stretford Bridge and the railway had gone.

The 'Potts'

The Potteries, Shrewsbury and North Wales Railway

The lure of the Irish Sea traffic lingered in the minds of railway promoters into the 1860s, even though Holyhead had been rail-served since 1850. One such plan, the Potteries, Shrewsbury and North Wales Railway (PSNWR), envisaged a railway that would run via the Tanat Valley and a substantial tunnel under the Berwyn Mountains to Porthmadog. Crossing the Lleyn Peninsula, a sheltered port near Nefyn would serve the sea crossing better than Holyhead.

In the event, it ran no further east than Shrewsbury and only just got into Wales. Ironically, its ultimate western extremity, the Nantmawr mineral line, was in Shropshire, though the line crossed the border briefly to get there. Like the Bishop's Castle Railway, it opened in 1866 and was soon in great financial difficulties. It had some fun and games with the bailiffs too. Also like the BCR, the railway struggled on through its hardships – to survive (on and off) for nearly 100 years.

The 'Potts' started life as the West Shropshire Mineral Railway, a line promoted by Richard France, whose limestone quarries around Llanymynech would provide much of the line's traffic. It was to have run from Westbury (on the Shrewsbury to Welshpool line) to Llanymynech and was authorized in 1862. As further opportunities were explored, the plans were changed (more Acts of Parliament …) – the line would be the Shrewsbury and North Wales Railway. It would extend westwards up the Tanat Valley, northwards to Nantmawr and Oswestry, and a branch from Melverley to Criggion would tap into yet more quarry traffic. At the eastern end, the railway would join the main line nearer Shrewsbury, at Redhill. This connection did not receive approval from Parliament (the GWR and LNWR did not want its trains in their station), so plans were formed for a line to a temporary station in Abbey Foregate, Shrewsbury, and a spur to the Wellington line.

In 1865, the Shrewsbury and Potteries Junction Railway was formed. Common interests led to amalgamation, creating the Potteries, Shrewsbury and North Wales Railway in July 1866, in an Act providing for the Tanat Valley line and extension to Porthmadog. It became known locally as the 'Potts'. Construction was well under way by now, and the railway was opened for traffic on 13 August 1866 between Shrewsbury Abbey station and Llanymynech. No fewer than nine Acts of Parliament had been obtained for this railway; as a result, it was thought to have been, at the time, the most expensive railway ever to have been built outside the major cities.

By 21 December 1866, the Potteries, Shrewsbury and North Wales Railway lay dormant, victim of its huge debts and sparse traffic. The bailiffs had arrived earlier in the month, on behalf of an unhappy (and unpaid) debenture holder and had seized a train. It was allowed to run (after some discussion) provided that a bailiff was on board. At Kinnerley, the guard generously provided a seat in a first-class compartment, in a coach at the back of the train provided specifically for his use. The bailiff was soon to discover that it was not coupled to the rest of the train …

A shareholders' meeting soon afterwards found that an operating loss had been made during the year, leading to the decision to suspend services and to sell some assets. Among those assets would be some of the line's rails. It had been built as a double-track railway, but already it was clear that a single line would suffice.

Services resumed two years later, in December 1868. During the next four years the Criggion (1871) and Nantmawr (1872) branches were opened, providing more traffic. In the 1870s, the railway made operating profits, but they could never be remotely sufficient to service a debt now approaching £1.5 million. By 1877, it was time to call in the Official Receiver. Maintenance suffered and in 1880 services were suspended by the Board of Trade because of the unsafe condition of the track.

The Shropshire Railways Company

With local support for the concept of a direct link from Shrewsbury to the Potteries, another Bill led to the formation of the Shropshire Railways Company. It would take over the old PSNWR, whose shareholders accepted £350,000 in the new company's shares. A further £150,000 would cover the costs of resuscitation.

The formal takeover was effective from 19 September 1890. Work progressed for around nine months – the whole main line needed to be resleepered, some timber bridges required replacement and Abbey Station needed raising above the Severn's flood level. Then on 15 July 1891, work stopped. It appears there may have been some dubious dealings between the contractor and the principal debenture holder, who was paying the contractor directly. Another receiver was appointed in November 1891 and the railway returned to dereliction and decay.

The Shropshire and Montgomeryshire Light Railway

In the years following the failure of the Shropshire Railways Co., there were two developments of great significance to minor railways in Britain. One was the appearance, on the minor railways stage, of the remarkable Colonel Stephens; the other was the passing of the Light Railways Act 1896.

Holman Fred Stephens attained the rank of Lieutenant Colonel during World War I, but is invariably referred to as 'Colonel', even in relation to his earlier activities. He was a railway civil engineer who developed a particular interest in the construction and operation of rural light railways. He first became involved with minor railways during the 1890s, opening the 3ft 0in (914mm) gauge Rye and Camber Tramway in 1895. His 'empire', managed from his offices in Tonbridge, Kent, eventually extended to some sixteen lines. As well as his Shropshire interests, two other well-known constituents of the empire were the Festiniog and Welsh Highland Railways.

The Colonel turned his attentions to the remains off the 'Potts' in 1907, applying for a Light Railway

year: the rails and chairs of the 'Potts' were found to be usable with new sleepers (again); bridges were checked and, where necessary, strengthened; stations were refurbished or replaced; and some new halts were constructed. On 13 April 1911, the line from Shrewsbury Abbey to Llanymynech was officially reopened. In the meantime, Melverley Viaduct on the Criggion branch needed rebuilding and the branch fully reopened in February the following year.

The main line ran entirely within the county of Shropshire – only that part of the Criggion branch south of the Severn is within Wales. The inclusion of 'Montgomeryshire' in the new company's title was partly in recognition of financial support from Montgomeryshire County Council.

Colonel Stephens' lines were noteworthy for their minimal budget make-do-and-mend approach. Their rolling stock was a delight for the eyes of the early twentieth-century railway enthusiast – and almost certainly quite the opposite for the travelling public. His locomotives and coaches were typically old and second-hand and the Shropshire and Montgomeryshire (S&M) was no exception. Probably its best-known locomotive, and today's only survivor from those times, is the quite remarkable *Gazelle*. It had been built in 1892 for a King's Lynn businessman who used it to travel around the Great Eastern Railway. A tiny 2–2–2 well tank, it was possibly the smallest standard-gauge steam locomotive ever built. Its wheels had wooden centres, it had no cab and its passengers

Order on 30 May. With agreement in place with the former Shropshire Railways Co. (from whom the line was to be leased), and empowered to raise £40,000 in loans, the Shropshire and Montgomeryshire's Light Railway Order was issued by the Board of Trade on 11 February 1909. The real work of reconstruction began the following

Originally built as a 2-2-2 in 1893, the Shropshire and Montgomeryshire's Dodman 0-4-2WT Gazelle stands at Llanymynech station on a special passenger working. Now preserved, it is one of the smallest standard-gauge locomotives ever built; 23 April 1939. PHOTOGRAPHER UNKNOWN/ KIDDERMINSTER RAILWAY MUSEUM

were carried on a bench seat above the coal bunker at the back.

Gazelle was bought by Stephens for the S&M in 1911. It was quickly converted to an 0-4-2, using the original 2ft 3in carrying wheels as patterns for the new driving wheels. With a rudimentary cab for the driver and another for the passengers, it was set to work on the Criggion branch. Later, a former London horse-tram was acquired; adapted for conventional (!) rail use, it became *Gazelle's* train.

Other locomotives included such delights as three former London and South Western Ilfracombe Goods 0-6-0s, three former London, Brighton and South Coast Terrier 0-6-0Ts, and the much-rebuilt *Severn* (formerly *Hecate*), built in or around 1853 as an 0-4-0 tender locomotive, by now running as an 0-4-2 saddle tank. Many carried names which, like *Hecate*, were generally classical in origin and (typical Col. Stephens) were recycled. One of the Terriers became the new *Hecate*; its class-mates were *Dido* and *Daphne*, while *Hesperus*, *Pyramus* and *Thisbe* were carried by the ex-LSWR 0-6-0s. The latter names *Pyramus* and *Thisbe* were first carried on two new 0-6-2Ts that Stephens bought new (an unusual event) for the S&M; they were too heavy for the lightly laid track and were sold on to the War Department.

Notwithstanding the seat in the cab of *Gazelle*, there was also an eclectic range of passenger vehicles. Four-wheeled, six-wheeled and bogie coaches of widely varying origin and antiquity saw service. All were second-hand, mostly from the Midland, the Plymouth, Devonport and South Western Junction (PD&SWJ) and the North Staffordshire. One particular 'celebrity' was the former PD&SWJ royal coach. Dating from 1848, it survived until the 1950s, by which time it was thoroughly rotten and woodworm-infested. Considered to be beyond restoration, it was broken up.

From 1923, the railway experimented with internal combustion, in the form of railcars built by Ford and Wolseley-Siddeley. Being essentially buses fitted with flanged railway wheels, they were single-ended and thus tended to be used in pairs, coupled back-to-back. Despite their modernity and economy, they were probably not the last word in passenger comfort. The Wolseleys lasted until 1929 (the body of one was rebuilt as a new coach for *Gazelle*, mounted on the former tram chassis); the Fords lasted into the 1930s.

Colonel Stephens died in October 1931. His assistant, W.H. Austen, took control of the 'empire', but the future was rather bleak in the face of growing road traffic. Just a year later, the passenger service beyond Melverley on the Criggion branch ended, due to fears about the safety of the viaduct over the Severn, though the stone traffic continued to run. In 1933, regular passenger services on the S&M ceased. Freight dwindled to a minimal level; only one engine was kept usable and the weeds grew. Remarkably, *Gazelle*, which had lain derelict at Kinnerley for some years, was overhauled and returned to service in 1937. In April 1938, an enthusiasts' special operated over the line, utilizing *Gazelle* and the Wolseley coach.

The Last Rebirth …

At the start of World War II, the railway was taken under Government control, though nothing really changed until 1941, when, apart from the Criggion branch, it was requisitioned by the War Department. The Department relaid the track, ballasted it properly and constructed a network of balloon loops along the line, with numerous sidings serving an array of military stores. More locomotives were brought in – a number of former GWR Dean Goods 0-6-0s saw service during the war years. Civilian goods traffic continued, including stone from Criggion. Melverley Viaduct had been damaged by floods in 1940, but remained in use – in latter years, the quarry company's Sentinel, being particularly light, hauled the traffic to Kinnerley Junction – at 5mph (8km/h) all the way.

After the war, the War Department gradually ran down its operations and use of the railway. In 1959, it closed its last remaining depot; the Criggion stone traffic finished in December of that year. Early in the new year the last scheduled train ran, followed on 20 March by a Stephenson Locomotive Society

Last day of the S&M: the SLS special of 20 March 1960 stands at Kinnerley Junction, in the charge of Austerity 0-6-0 no. 193, which later entered preservation. Spending several years on the Severn Valley Railway, it received the name Shropshire. H. GRABNER, COURTESY SHREWSBURY RAILWAY HERITAGE TRUST

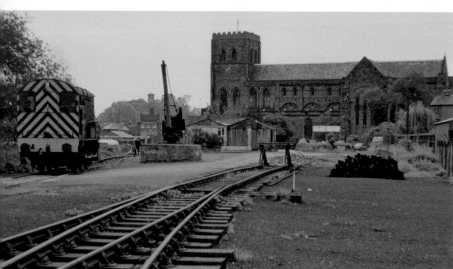

The remains of Shrewsbury Abbey station, seen on 16 June 1977. 08 112 is reversing away from the oil depot siding. The former station platform, now devoid of track, can just be seen beneath the truncated gable of the Abbey's south front. STEVE PRICE

BELOW: *Hookagate: the tracks on the left are on the formation of the 'Potts' – the rail welding depot was established on the site of the MoD exchange sidings after the final closure of the S&M; 26 October 1978.* STEVE PRICE

special. On 31 March, it was formally handed over to BR and within a couple of years the track had been lifted.

Fragments remained – at Hookagate a long-welded rail depot was established on the site of the War Department's exchange sidings. The nine half-mile (800m) sidings received trains of 60ft (18m) rails that were welded into lengths up to 900ft (275m). The depot remained in operation until 1986. In Shrewsbury, a spur was constructed from the Severn Valley line to provide access to the former Abbey station, which remained open for freight and oil traffic, the latter continuing until 1988. The track was removed the following year and the site has been redeveloped, with much of

Former Cambrian Railways 0-6-0 no. 14, now GWR no. 898, is shunting on the Nantmawr branch on 7 May 1935. This remnant of the ill-fated Potteries, Shrewsbury and North Wales Railway, which became part of the CR and GWR, still exists in the hands of preservation. V.R. WEBSTER/ KIDDERMINSTER RAILWAY MUSEUM

the land around the station area now occupied by a car park. The station building and platform have been rescued from final oblivion by the Shrewsbury Railway Heritage Trust.

One final short length remains of the Nantmawr mineral branch. When the original 'Potts' failed, the railway from Llanymynech to Nantmawr was leased by the Cambrian Railways in order to access the valuable stone traffic. Other than the short length incorporated into the Llanfyllin branch in 1894, the line between Llanymynech and Blodwell Junction became disused in 1925 and was later lifted, as the last mile or so to the Nantmawr quarries could by then be accessed from the Tanat Valley line at Blodwell. It remained in use until the early 1970s, but the track was not lifted and it has since been taken on by preservationists.

The Snailbeach District Railways

The Shropshire and Montgomeryshire Railway was not Colonel Stephens' only interest in the railways of Shropshire – in 1923 another minor railway came to his attention.

Snailbeach lies to the west of the Stiperstones ridge, at its northern end. Lead is known to have been mined in the vicinity in Roman times. One of several mines in the area, the Snailbeach Mine was the biggest, and was thought to be one of the richest in Europe in terms of lead per acre.

The railway, a little over 3 miles (5km) in length, was built in 1877, linking the Snailbeach mines to

Pontesbury, on the Minsterley branch, where there were trans-shipment sidings. Its unusual gauge, 2ft 4in (711mm), was almost exactly half standard gauge. So was the 2ft 4½in (724mm) gauge of the Glyn Valley Tramway, perhaps 20 miles (32km) away. The same family – Henry Dennis and his son Henry Dyke Dennis – were involved in the engineering and operation of both railways. When the Glyn Valley was reconstructed for the use of steam locomotives, it borrowed and used (despite the slight difference in gauge) two Snailbeach locomotives.

The trick did not work the other way round. In 1905, a quarry near Habberley was opened by the Ceiriog Granite Company, closely associated with the Glyn Valley Tramway. The Glyn Valley lent one of its locomotives, 0-4-2T *Sir Theodore* to Snailbeach to handle the extra traffic, but the ½in (13mm) difference made it impossible to use and the company bought a new locomotive, a fairly substantial 0-6-0T built by Bagnall of Stafford. Delivered in 1907, it was named *Dennis*.

Like its near neighbour, the Bishop's Castle Railway, there was an indirect connection from the main line to the Snailbeach terminus and mines. Running to a headshunt at Crowsnest, the line then reversed into the mining complex. Similarly, the line's Act authorized construction of further lines that were never built, in this case beyond Crowsnest to lead mines near Pennerley.

The railway was prosperous at first, paying 3 per cent dividends, but when the Tankerville Great

Snailbeach locomotive shed in 1936: 0-4-2T no. 2 (Kerr Stuart 802 of 1902) stands beside Baldwin no. 3, built in 1918. The remains of the Bagnall *Dennis* can be seen to the right of the shed. DON POWELL COLLECTION/KIDDERMINSTER RAILWAY MUSEUM

Consols Company's mine closed in 1884, annual freight tonnages more than halved. There were, however, still several other lead mines in operation in this part of the county and in 1890 plans were drawn up for the Shropshire Minerals Light Railway. This would extend the 2ft 4in metals considerably, via Pennerley and Rock House Mine to Gatten Lodge, with a branch from Pennerley to mines at Gravels. It failed to raise the necessary capital – mine owners knew that the industry was dying. Its construction would have been difficult and costly, but it would have resulted in the longest such railway in England.

By 1898, the railway was operating at a loss. Lead traffic continued to dwindle and had virtually ended when *Dennis* was purchased. Although valuable for a time, stone traffic had also passed its peak within a few years. Some new traffic had been generated from 1900 by the Halvans Company, which extracted barytes and other minerals from mine waste. Barytes was also worked from the former lead mines, providing further post-lead traffic.

The onset of World War I brought greater financial problems, including the end of the stone traffic. The little traffic remaining – some coal and timber – was at best intermittent. Nevertheless, Colonel Stephens saw some hope for the line, taking on responsibility for the line – and its debts – from 1 January 1923.

Stephens quickly set about renovating the line. Track was resleepered and, for much of its length, relaid with heavier rail. Three locomotives were purchased – a 1902 Kerr Stuart 0-4-2T Skylark and two ex-WD Baldwin 4-6-0Ts, refurbished by Bagnall of Stafford after war service. The wagon stock was similarly augmented.

In 1927, a roadstone quarry opened beside the line at Callow Hill, not quite 1 mile (1.6km) from the Pontesbury interchange with the Minsterley branch; it was taken into County Council ownership in 1930. This traffic could not be hugely lucrative on a mileage basis, but there was enough of it to ensure that the railway was moderately prosperous for a number of years. During this period the light engine mileage, from the loco shed at Snailbeach, far exceeded the traffic mileage. Light engines were the only movements on the greater part of the railway when the last traffic from the Snailbeach area ended in the 1940s.

By 1946, the locomotives had all become unusable, so the Callow Hill traffic was handled in an unorthodox manner – a farm tractor, straddling the narrow-gauge rails, was used to haul and shunt the wagons. The locomotives remained, increasingly derelict, at the loco shed until they were cut up in 1950. Shropshire County Council had leased the Callow Hill to Pontesbury section of the line from April 1947 and the remaining track was taken up, apart from in the vicinity of the loco shed, where some lengths remain. When road access was provided to Callow Hill Quarry in 1959, the last stretch of railway became disused and was lifted. One remaining wagon has been restored and can be seen today in the old loco shed, which, along with other buildings and exhibits at Snailbeach, is maintained and managed by the Shropshire Mines Trust on behalf of the County Council. The great white spoil heaps that were a distinctive feature of the local landscape were sealed and landscaped by the County Council in the 1990s.

The Cleobury Mortimer and Ditton Priors Light Railway

The Minsterley branch was in the valley of the Rea Brook; another Rea Brook rises perhaps 15 miles (24km) to the south-east, near the village of Ditton Priors, becoming the River Rea as it flows southwards. That valley also bore the metals of a railway.

Within southern Shropshire lies a rural area of the kind that the Light Railways Act had been intended for. At the end of the nineteenth century a large, roughly triangular area was delineated by railways, mostly byways: the Severn Valley line from Bewdley to Buildwas; the line from Buildwas via Much Wenlock to Craven Arms; then, a few miles down the North and West, the railway from Woofferton via Cleobury Mortimer to Bewdley.

Inside the triangle, a short mineral line from Ludlow served the stone quarries on Titterstone Clee; there was no such provision for its more northerly neighbour, Shropshire's highest hill, Brown Clee. Today, the quarrying would be unthinkable, but over 100 years ago, the hard dhustone around its summit at Abdon Burf was a valuable resource to be exploited. Brown Clee lies roughly in the centre of the triangle and, in 1900, plans were prepared for a railway to serve the region. Opening in 1908, it made a junction with the GWR at Cleobury Mortimer and followed the River Rea northwards to Ditton Priors. Here, a standard-gauge rope-worked incline was constructed by the Abdon Clee Quarrying Company, taking rails to the summit plateau of the hill, where 2ft 0in (610mm) gauge tramways ran to the quarry faces.

The Cleobury Mortimer and Ditton Priors (CM&DP) Light Railway was the only line entirely within Shropshire to be constructed under the Light Railways legislation. Like the other minor

The locomotive shed at Snailbeach survived, along with several other buildings dating from mining days. Inside is a restored Snailbeach Railway wagon. The rails around the shed area were not lifted when the line closed – the wagon could thus be pushed outside the shed for photography; 9 June 2013.

lines, it developed unfulfilled plans for extensions. One involved a steeply graded link to the Severn Valley line near Bridgnorth; another examined the possibility of a more northerly Severn Valley link, at Coalport. A third would take rails to Presthope, on the Wenlock Edge line south of Much Wenlock. Relatively low construction costs and easier gradients made it the most likely, but World War I put an end to such ideas.

Two new locomotives were purchased for the railway. Built by Manning Wardle of Leeds (1734 and 1735 of 1908), the outside-cylindered 0–6–0 saddle tanks became the railway's nos 1 and 2, bearing the names *Burwarton* and *Cleobury*. When the CM&DP became part of the GWR, after the grouping, they became GWR nos 29 and 28 (in that order). Inevitably, they were 'Great Westernized' and were later rebuilt as pannier tanks. They lasted until the early years of BR. There were also industrial locomotives at Ditton Priors, property of the

Cleobury and its train of four ex-North London Railway coaches are seen passing the locomotive shed at Cleobury Town. Of unknown date, the photo was clearly taken before the locomotive was rebuilt as a pannier tank at Swindon in late 1930. *G.E.S. PARKER COLLECTION/KIDDERMINSTER RAILWAY MUSEUM*

quarry company. One, another Manning Wardle, no. 313 of 1888 *Kingswood*, had been used in construction of the CM&DP.

In addition to carrying stone from Brown Clee, the CM&DP would, for nearly twenty years, benefit from quarrying on Titterstone Clee. Most of the hill's stone left by the inclines to Bitterley, thence to the main line at Ludlow, but the quarries developed at Magpie Hill, on the north-eastern flank of Titterstone Clee, were somewhat remote from the railhead. In 1909, a 3½-mile (5.6km) aerial ropeway was constructed to take stone down to the CM&DP station at Detton Ford. The stone was worked out by 1928 and the ropeway subsequently dismantled for scrap; the concrete bases, four to each pylon, remain and can easily be seen on the upper part of the route.

Like the Bishop's Castle and the S&M, the CM&DP's natural life drew to a close in the late 1930s. When Abdon Clee quarries closed in 1937, the railway's days were numbered. The passenger service finished in September 1938, but freight limped on until World War II began a year later. In common with the S&M, the military authorities saw potential in the land around its terminus. Ditton Priors became a most unlikely naval establishment, in the form of a Royal Naval Armament Depot. Completed by mid-1941, small 'dumps' had already quietly been established beside the stations en route. During the war, the daily freight train was, in effect, a daily ammunition train, moving highly explosive goods up and down the line. The locomotives working the line were fitted with spark-arresting chimneys, for obvious reasons. Nevertheless, they handed over their traffic to flame-proofed diesels in the Ditton Priors transfer sheds.

Trains continued to run after the war, gradually becoming less frequent. They ran 'as required', sometimes as often as three times a week, but more usually weekly. From 30 September 1957, the Admiralty took over the whole branch and for eight years their Ruston and Hornsby diesels trundled to Cleobury Mortimer and back. By 1965, the Admiralty traffic between Cleobury and Bewdley was the only traffic remaining on the Woofferton to Bewdley line. In that year, the Admiralty announced that it would cease operations at Ditton Priors. Normal traffic ended at Easter; some equipment was subsequently moved out by rail, but by June the depot was closed and the locomotives had gone, by road.

24 September 1938: the last train prepares to leave Ditton Priors in a fine autumn drizzle. The former Cleobury is now just plain no. 28 – and is now a pannier tank. *K. BEDDOES COLLECTION/KIDDERMINSTER RAILWAY MUSEUM*

There was a possibility that the line might see further use. It was considered by the preservationists, but dropped in favour of the Severn Valley. The US Army set up a temporary dump on the Ditton Priors site in 1967 and there was speculation that the branch might have a future, but it was not to be. Some track lifting had already taken place between Bewdley and Cleobury, and the MoD had sold off the line between Cleobury and Ditton Priors. The Americans used road vehicles to service their facility; by the time they left the site, the track of the Cleobury Mortimer and Ditton Priors Light Railway had gone.

The Tanat Valley Light Railway

One further minor line should be mentioned. Born, like the CM&DP, of the Light Railways Act, it was in many respects a classic rural Welsh byway – but of the almost 20-mile (32km) journey from Oswestry to the terminus at Llangynog, the first 8 miles (13km) were in Shropshire.

The scheme received its Light Railway Order in September 1897, the ceremonial start of construction following some two years later when sufficient capital was in place. The first part of the route from Oswestry was already in existence, in the form of the Cambrian main line south to Llynclys Junction, thence the Porthywaen mineral line. Tanat Valley metals began at Porthywaen, then used a short stretch of the former 'Potts' Nantmawr branch, joining it at Nantmawr Junction, and diverging perhaps a quarter of a mile (0.4km) further west at Blodwell Junction . The line then made its lonely way up the valley to its terminus, nestling deep within the Berwyn Mountains. Llangynog was a potential source of slate and granite traffic for the railway – but, by the time the railway opened, the slate industry was in decline.

As with so many similar schemes, the construction and opening of the line were not without difficulties. When it finally opened, in January 1904, it was already in serious financial trouble. The cost of construction came to more than £92,000 – double the 1897 figure. Bankrupt, the Official Receiver was brought in within months and the railway ran in receivership until it was taken over by the Cambrian in 1921. It remained a part of the main-line network until closure. Its Light Railway origins meant that its passenger services retained a 'minor lines' flavour. Small, light locomotives hauled trains of, usually, antiquated four-wheeled coaches, until they were withdrawn in 1951. It was the first part of Shropshire's BR passenger network to close.

Standing beside Oswestry shed on 6 August 1935 is ex-Cambrian Railways 2-4-0T no. 1196 (CR no. 58) with a Tanat Valley train. H.F. WHEELLER

CHAPTER 6

Industry

Shropshire is a rural county, despite its unique position at the start of the Industrial Revolution, and the current status of Telford as a significant manufacturing centre. There are no longer any industrial railways or locomotives active in the county; nevertheless, industrial railways have their place in this book. When most of the country's goods moved by rail, any business with a substantial need for raw materials and/or a substantial output of finished products would use a railway. At the end of BR steam, there were still thousands of industrial premises where locomotives were used and the large number still using steam began to attract the attention of enthusiasts.

Standard-gauge industrial railways added interest to many rail journeys. Interesting-looking sidings burrowed into dark smoky corners; diminutive locomotives wrestled with rakes of wagons, or simmered in sidings beside the main line.

Narrow-gauge industrial railways were less obvious. Some developed from early plateways; many were built using surplus materials – track, locomotives and wagons – left over from World War I. Typically of 2ft 0in (610mm) gauge, as seen at the Llanforda Hall filter beds near Oswestry, or the Westbury Brick and Tile Co. beside the Shrewsbury to Welshpool railway, Shropshire's examples ranged from 4ft 0in (1,220mm) gauge (unusual) to 1ft 3in (381mm) gauge (rope-worked).

Sentinel of Shrewsbury was widely known as a builder of industrial railway locomotives, but in the nineteenth century a number of locomotives were built by the Lilleshall company at Oakengates.

The railways below are not intended to form an exhaustive list, merely a representative sample of the better-known lines. Industrial railways, especially those built to the small gauges, have existed in the most unlikely places and it is possible that some escaped all documentation.

Sentinel

The Glasgow engineering company Alley and MacLellan, established in 1875, moved to the Sentinel Works in Polmadie in 1880. In 1903, the company took over Simpson and Bibby, a Horsehay, Shropshire-based manufacturer of steam lorries, and moved that business to Polmadie. It then developed a new steam lorry, which was launched under the brand name 'Sentinel'. Around 1915, steam lorry production was moved back to Shropshire, this time to Shrewsbury, forming a new company, the Sentinel Waggon Works Ltd, to handle this new venture.

The Sentinel name is justly famed for its steam road vehicles, but the mechanism employed proved more than suitable for railway use. The vertical water-tube boiler could be steamed relatively

*An early Sentinel (8098 of 1930)
is seen in action at Chatwood Safe
and Engineering Co. Ltd, Shrewsbury.
The vertical boiler is in the cab, the
cylinders inside the 'smokebox' at the
front. The exposed external chain
drive would not be allowed today.*
J.A. PEDEN PHOTOGRAPH, COPYRIGHT
INDUSTRIAL RAILWAY SOCIETY

quickly and, when fitted to a suitable railway chassis, the vertical cylinders and chain drive resulted in a small but powerful shunting locomotive, albeit one with a low maximum speed. Fitted with gears, higher speeds (but lower tractive effort) could be attained. A particular advantage of the design was the relatively steady drawbar pull, whereas a conventional steam shunter would impart a certain amount of to-and-fro motion.

Sentinel steam locomotives became a reasonably familiar sight amongst the smaller industrial users, but were also adopted by some of the main-line companies for the same sort of work. The LNER had nearly fifty; dating from the early days of the LNER, many survived to see use by British Railways. One, former Departmental no. 59, previously 68153, is preserved at the Middleton Railway in Leeds.

Sentinel's steam railcars utilized a gear ratio that was appropriate for passenger service speed. Again,

the LNER was an enthusiastic adopter. After trials in the north-east, a further eighty were purchased from 1925 to 1932. Early examples were formed of a coach articulated to an engine unit; later models used a rigid coach body with the engine and mechanism at one end, connected to a power bogie by flexible gearing. One unit, named *Phenomena* (most of the railcars bore names) consisted of two coaches articulated to a single central power bogie. It achieved a speed of 64mph (103km/h) whilst on trial. All had been withdrawn from service by February 1948 and none was preserved. However, a three-car articulated unit built for Egyptian Railways in 1951 was bought by the Sentinel Trust in 1985. It is undergoing restoration at the Quainton Road Railway Centre in Buckinghamshire.

The early Sentinel shunters were perhaps rather quaint and 'boxy' in appearance. Later examples, resembling diesel shunters, looked 'modern', but

*These two Sentinels stand under an arch of the railway viaduct
at the Coalbrookdale Museum of Iron. Both are rebuilds, dating
from 1925, of conventional locomotives. The complete S6155 was
originally an 1873 Manning Wardle, while partially dismantled
S6185, a rebuild of Coalbrookdale's own no. 6, displays the vertical
cylinders and remains of the vertical boiler; February 1980.*

could be operated and maintained by steam-age skills. Nevertheless, it became clear in the post-war years that steam did not have a long-term future. From 1947, Sentinel began the manufacture of diesel lorries and buses, but, despite being well-engineered, they were not a success.

The last big order for steam lorries had been in 1950, when a batch was sent to Argentina. Lorry production ended in 1956 and the change from steam to diesel locomotive manufacture, and ultimately the end of locomotive building in Shropshire, began. Rolls-Royce acquired the business, with the intention of producing diesel engines (as opposed to locomotives). Existing orders would be completed and the last steam locomotive emerged from the works in 1958. However, it was realized that a diesel locomotive, built using Rolls-Royce engines on a steam chassis, might also build upon the steamers' success. The following year, diesel locomotive 10001 was completed. It was the first of a large batch of locomotives that went to the iron and steel industry in the north-east of England. The smaller locomotives continued to use the efficient and relatively inexpensive chain drive of the steamers, with hydraulic transmission, but when larger and more powerful models were developed, it became necessary to switch to side rods between the driving wheels.

For many years, Sentinels were tested on Shropshire's railways. Steam locomotives and the very first diesels ran on the Shropshire and Montgomeryshire line; after the latter closed, the remains of the Severn Valley line and the Minsterley branch would also see Shrewsbury-built locomotives under test.

The last Sentinel was no. 10186 of 1964. The next locomotive, 10187, was a Rolls-Royce. A notable new design was the Steelman Class, a six-wheeled, 600hp diesel-hydraulic that should have been a big seller. However, events in the outside world meant that only a handful were built. British Railways had developed a class of 650hp 0-6-0 diesel-hydraulic locomotives for heavy shunting and short-trip freight working. Fifty-six were built at Swindon in 1964 and 1965, but the work for which they were designed had more or less disappeared within a few years. All had been withdrawn by April 1969, but only eight went for scrap; the remainder were sold (at very advantageous prices) to industry, notably the National Coal Board (NCB) in the north-east and the steel industry in the east Midlands. Corby might have been the home of a large Steelman fleet; instead, it became home to around thirty of the ex-BR locomotives.

At about the same time as Rolls-Royce locomotives began to emerge from Shrewsbury, the company was expanding the facilities at its subsidiary, Thomas Hill (Rotherham) Ltd, whom it had taken over in 1963. Thomas Hill was already closely linked with Sentinel, acting as sales agents for the company as well as selling its own Vanguard locomotives. It had worked with Rolls-Royce on that company's diesel locomotive designs and was sole agent for diesel locomotive sales. Over a three-year period from 1968, the locomotive business was transferred to Thomas Hill's Kilnhurst works and locomotive building in Shropshire came to an end.

Some of Sentinel's earliest locomotives, such as the pair at the Museum of Iron in Coalbrookdale,

Unofficially named Princess, 9603 of 1956 for Dorman Long, Middlesbrough, was the biggest locomotive ever built by Sentinel. It is seen here apparently on test at the Shrewsbury works. With a tractive effort, in low gear, of 52,000lb (23,600kg), it was more powerful than a GWR King or an LMS Duchess, but somewhat slower. Its life at Dorman Long was short – replaced by (Sentinel) diesels, it was scrapped at the Redcar Works circa 1966. J.A. PEDEN PHOTOGRAPH, COPYRIGHT INDUSTRIAL RAILWAY SOCIETY

were rebuilds, with vertical boilers and vertical cylinders, of conventional locomotives. The story turned full circle when Thomas Hill began locomotive engineering – many of its early diesels were rebuilds of Sentinel steam locomotives.

The Midland Wagon Company

For a number of years in the pre-grouping period, trams, railway carriages and wagons were built in Shrewsbury. The Abbey Works was located immediately south of the Rea Brook, between the Hereford line north of Coleham locomotive shed and the Abbey station of the old 'Potts' railway. For a time it was connected to both railways. The business was purchased by the Midland Wagon Company, of Birmingham, in 1877, which very shortly afterwards changed its name to the Midland Railway-Carriage and Wagon Company (no connection with the Midland Railway Company).

In 1912, the company began to use its new factory at Washwood Heath and production at Shrewsbury ended. The Washwood Heath factory continued in production for many more years – it became Metropolitan Cammell, whose diesel multiple units could be seen in Shropshire from late steam days until they were replaced by the second-generation units. The works closed in 2005. Some of its tram cars are still in existence; at least one Blackpool vehicle and a couple from the Giant's Causeway Tramway.

The Lilleshall Company

Sentinel's products are well-known in railway circles; the Lilleshall Company's locomotives less so. Built over a period from 1862 to 1888, none survived, despite their longevity. *Constance*, an 0-4-0

saddle tank that worked the company's railways from 1865, was scrapped in 1957. *Rawnsley* was built as a 2-2-2 express locomotive for the Paris exhibition of 1867, but remained unsold. After conversion to an 0-6-0 saddle tank it was sold to the Cannock and Rugeley Collieries at Rawnsley, Staffordshire, and remained there until it was scrapped in 1962.

The company was formed in 1802, replacing a partnership established in 1764 by Granville Leveson-Gower – the second Earl Gower. His ancestors had purchased the Lilleshall estate from Henry VIII and his descendants remained involved in the company for many years. Its independent existence only ended in 2001 when Lilleshall plc was acquired by Wyko Industrial Services Ltd.

The Lilleshall Company was not primarily a manufacturer of locomotives – it was much more than that. The estate contained substantial reserves of coal, ironstone, limestone and fireclay. Its private railway ran, at its greatest extent, from Lubstree Wharf, on a branch of the Shrewsbury Canal near The Humbers, Donnington, to the GWR main line at Hollinswood, and beyond to pits such as Stafford Colliery, now vanished beneath Stafford Park industrial estate. It also connected to the Coalport branch, at Oakengates, and to the Wellington–Newport line at Donnington. A straight line would have been about 4 miles (6.5km), but it was not at all straight and there were many connections to various furnaces, brickworks, mines and tips, plus the substantial engineering works at New Yard,

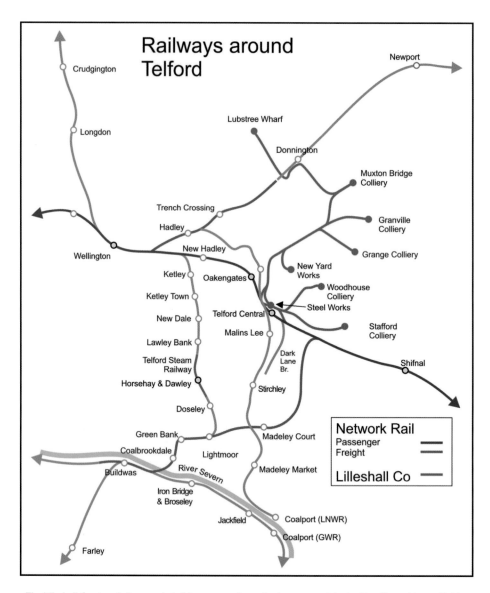

The Lilleshall Company's lines, at their fullest extent, formed quite a network in the East Shropshire coalfield. The map depicts that network, simplified for clarity, in relation to the main-line network past and present in the Telford area.

St George's. Company records claim 11¼ miles (18km) of running lines and a further 14¼ miles (23km) of siding, as well as numerous narrow-gauge railways.

Some of the mines had narrow-gauge surface tramways, on which pit tubs could be moved. The Old Lodge furnaces were fed by a 3ft 0in (914mm) gauge railway, for which two locomotives were built by the company in 1869. Those furnaces closed around 1890, superseded by the Priorslee furnaces and ironworks – a steelworks, in fact, from 1882 until 1925. Iron-making and rolling continued until 1959, soon after closure in late 1958 of most of the company's railway.

Constance *was the Lilleshall Company's longest-serving locomotive. Named after the daughter of the second Duke of Sutherland, she was built in 1865 (works no. 89) and lived on the company's railway until scrapping in early 1957. She may have been a little like the proverbial broom, having had new frames and at least two new boilers during her long life.* IRONBRIDGE GORGE MUSEUM TRUST

The 18in (457mm)-gauge chain-operated plateway at the Lilleshall Company's Donnington Brickworks. The chain locating in the slot on the upper end of the wagons can be seen. IRONBRIDGE GORGE MUSEUM TRUST

The Lilleshall Company's Priorslee Furnaces are seen in an aerial photograph thought to date from around 1950. The tracks leading out of the bottom of the picture led to Hollinswood yard; the GWR main line is just off to the left. The site is now occupied by Telford's Central Park, an estate of modern commercial premises. The A5 trunk road running across the top of the picture and St Peter's Church, top right, provide markers to locate the scene. IRONBRIDGE GORGE MUSEUM TRUST

In addition to those built by the company, a wonderful variety of bought-in locomotives saw service on the company's lines – some new, others second-hand. There were a few ex-main-line locomotives – three ex-South Wales 0–6–2Ts were obtained in the early 1930s and a 1901-built GWR pannier tank was bought in 1950. Other locomotives, from several different builders, were mostly 0–4–0 and 0–6–0 saddle tanks, but there was an unusual 0–4–4T, a 1902-built Hudswell Clarke. Obtained from Armstrong Whitworth around 1919, it lasted until 1934.

Coal

Granville

The Lilleshall Company's numerous mines were (with the exception of Hope, near Wrexham) located in the area served by the company's railway system, in the East Shropshire coalfield. Most were worked for fireclay and ironstone as well as coal – some were originally sunk for ironstone. Two, Grange and Granville, survived to be nationalized in 1947. Grange Mine was connected underground to Granville in 1952 and ceased to function as a separate entity, though the shaft and winding gear were retained. Granville closed in May 1979, with the last train to the exchange sidings at Donnington running in October of that year. The site of Granville has been cleared and landscaped as a part of Granville Country Park, though the course of much of the railway network is still evident. The route of the line to the exchange sidings has been used by a new road, the B5060.

Much of the output from Granville in later years went for electricity generation, with the power station at Ironbridge being the main customer. A straight line drawn between Granville and Ironbridge would be about 7 miles (11km), but coal had to travel more than double that distance. Two reversals were required between the Colliery and the exchange sidings; one, at Muxton, was eliminated by a short new stretch of line in the mid-1950s. On the main line, trains would have to reverse again in Wellington and a further reversal

was needed at Madeley Junction to gain access to the Ironbridge line.

Before nationalization, the lines were operated by Lilleshall locomotives. A former Taff Vale 0–6–2 tank of 1895 was transferred with the pit to the NCB, but saw little work. Similarly, an 0–6–0 saddle tank transferred in 1950 did not last long. It had been built by the Lilleshall Company in 1869. The NCB bought some new locomotives – Barclay 0–4–0ST, no. 2246 of 1948 and Hunslet 3771 of 1952, an Austerity type 0–6–0ST. The latter became Granville's no. 5. Locomotives transferred to the Colliery included *The Colonel*, a 1914-built Hudswell Clarke 0–6–0ST, which arrived in 1963, and Hunslet Austerity type no. 3776 of 1952 arrived in 1968. Becoming Granville's no. 8, it was already a much travelled locomotive and later worked at West Cannock no. 5 Colliery and Bickershaw in Lancashire. Happily, it lives on in preservation at the Embsay and Bolton Abbey Steam Railway in the Yorkshire Dales.

In 1969, two new Hunslet diesels arrived and steam working ended. Remaining to the end at Granville, they were joined in the late 1970s by another Hunslet diesel from West Cannock no. 5.

Kemberton

There were many pits further south within the Coalbrookdale coalfield, including those mentioned in the first chapter, around Broseley.

The Madeley Wood Company, like the Lilleshall Company, operated mines, blast furnaces, brickworks and tileworks, in the southern part of what is now Telford. The remains of its blast furnaces are preserved within the Blists Hill Museum complex, as are the remains of the Blists Hill Mine, where a stationary steam engine (from Milburgh Pit, south of the Severn) is demonstrated raising and lowering a cage in the original mine shaft. Its last pit, Kemberton, was nationalized in 1947 and lasted a further twenty years. It did not use surface locomotives; instead, narrow-gauge rope-worked tramways ran to the screens beside the Madeley Junction to Lightmoor railway. Similarly, wagons were moved by means of ropes and gravity to and from the exchange sidings, which were worked

by main-line locomotives. Five 2ft 0in (610mm) gauge flame-proofed Ruston and Hornsby diesels worked underground from the mid-1950s until closure. One of these left to work elsewhere in 1956, but the others were abandoned underground at closure. Some of the relatively modern surface buildings remain in use to this day, within Telford's Halesfield industrial estate.

Forest of Wyre Coalfield

In effect a continuation southwards of the Coalbrookdale coalfield, there were several mines in this area – some in Worcestershire, others in Shropshire. Within the county, the Highley Mining Company's pits are of interest.

Highley Mine was sunk in 1878, to the south of the village, and connected to the Severn Valley line below by a rope-worked incline. Horses were used at the top level in the vicinity of the pit; it is thought that a steam locomotive may have been used there at one time.

The mine's workings gradually extended eastwards, under the river towards Alveley, where a new shaft was developed from 1935. It opened fully in 1939; the following year, winding of coal at Highley ceased. Initially, Alveley's coal was taken to the exchange sidings across the river by a narrow-gauge rope-worked tramway, replaced in 1960 by an aerial ropeway. With demand in decline, the last coal was wound from this modern colliery in November 1968 and it was officially closed the following January, bringing an end to BR's use of the Severn Valley line north of Bewdley.

Alveley Colliery used 2ft 6in (762mm) gauge flame-proof battery-electric locomotives underground; 2ft 6in gauge diesels, a Lister and, later, a Ruston and Hornsby, were used in the surface stockyard.

Two other significant mines were owned by the Highley Mining Company, Kinlet and Billingsley. Attempts were made to develop a mine at Billingsley in the late nineteenth century – in 1880, work began on a railway to the pit from the Severn Valley line, following the course of the Borle Brook, but it was soon abandoned. Kinlet was actually much nearer Highley than the village whose name it bore, lying just south of the Borle Brook, a little under a mile from the Severn Valley line. It was connected to the latter by a standard-gauge railway, which followed the route planned for the Billingsley line. The Billingsley Colliery Company was formed in 1910; three years later, it had completed the railway to the mine. Never a great success, the mine was bought by the Highley Company in 1915 and closed in 1922. Nor was Kinlet an easy mine to work; proving impossible to mechanize, it was closed from 1937.

Both Billingsley and Kinlet used standard-gauge steam locomotives. Billingsley had a second-hand Peckett (no. 599, built in 1895); Kinlet took delivery of the brand-new Barclay 0–6–0ST (no. 782 of 1896), now preserved as a static exhibit at Blists Hill, and later acquired a couple of second-hand locomotives, a Hawthorn Leslie (3424 of 1919) and, just before closure, a Hudswell Clarke (1401 of 1920). Evidence of the colliery railway remains to this day. The trackbed is obvious, partly a public footpath,

and some bridges and other structures remain. The former incline from Highley Mine to the exchange sidings is also in use as a footpath.

Ifton

Observant drivers on the A5, just south of Chirk, may notice the remains of a railway embankment that once crossed the road. It was part of the 2½ mile (4km) private railway that once carried coal from Shropshire's biggest mine to exchange sidings beside the main line at Weston Rhyn.

Ifton, in the St Martin's district a few miles north-east of Oswestry, was the last operational pit in the Oswestry coalfield, a southwards extension of the Denbighshire coalfield, and was only just within the county. Ifton and Brynkinalt collieries lay either side of the border river, the Ceiriog. The Gertrude Shaft at Ifton was originally intended

A cab ride for the photographer – the driver's eye view over the side tank and boiler of Hudswell Clarke Unity *(1587 of 1927) at Ifton Colliery, St Martin's, on 23 November 1966.* BERWYN STEVENS

to be additional to the Brynkinalt Shaft, but the mine owners, W.Y. Craig and Co. of Preesgweene, soon realized that the Ifton site would be easier to operate.

The railway was complete by mid-1921, with a locomotive shed and a small wagon works at Weston Rhyn. The two pits were connected under-ground from 1923 and five years later Brynkinalt ceased to be used for winding coal; it was retained for ventilation and access.

In latter years, four steam locomotives operated at Ifton. Two were 0-4-0 saddle tanks for shunt-ing; *Spider*, a 1905-built Hawthorn Leslie (no. 2623) and *Hornet*, a Peckett (no. 1935) built in 1937. The other two locomotives were much larger 0-6-0 side tanks, acquired for working the steeply graded branch line. Both were Hudswell Clarke machines, *Richboro* (1243) dating from 1917, while *Unity* (1587) was built in 1927.

Hornet came to Ifton from nearby Black Park Colliery when it closed. It had been constructed to fit within some tight clearances at Black Park and was barely taller than the wagons it shunted. After Ifton's closure in 1968, the 'cut-down Peckett' worked at Bersham Colliery near Wrexham. One of the last steam locomotives to operate in normal (industrial) service, it retired in 1980, but lives on at the Ribble Steam Railway, Preston. *Richboro* was

On the same day as the previous picture, Unity *is making heavy weather of a rake of loaded wagons at Ifton Colliery.*
BERWYN STEVENS

sent to Gresford Colliery when Ifton closed and has also survived, finding its way, via Llangollen, Wooler and Bo'ness, to the Aln Valley Railway in Northumberland.

Ironbridge Power Station

The cooling towers of Ironbridge Power Station have been a distinctive feature of the local land-scape since the B station was built in the late 1960s. Older residents will remember the six chimneys of A station that stood nearby on the riverside site. Known then as Buildwas Power Station, it was officially opened on 13 October 1932 by the West Midlands Joint Electricity Authority. Its three boilers, each with a tall chimney, supplied steam to a single 50MW generator. Later extended, by 1939 there was a second boiler house, another three chimneys and a total nominal output of 200MW.

One reason for the site's selection was its prox-imity to a number of collieries, but being located beside a minor railway crossroads, coal could be delivered from several directions.

In November 1962, the Ministry of Power author-ized a second, bigger power station. Work began on the site in 1963 and some six years later it began supplying electricity to the National Grid. By this time, most of the local railways had closed and, henceforth, all deliveries of fuel by rail would come along the line from Madeley Junction. The track of the Severn Valley line to Shrewsbury, closed in September 1963, remained in situ until certain heavy materials and equipment, notably a long boiler component, had been delivered.

Like several others across the country, Ironbridge B was designed for 'merry-go-round' operation, but with insufficient land in the valley for a balloon loop, locomotives would have to run around their trains before discharging.

The A station remained in regular use until the mid-1970s. Generation was then scaled back to win-ter-only, until its last use in January 1978. A little over five years later, the station had been demol-ished and the site cleared. Its steam shunters were virtually redundant once it had gone, although they

No.3 (Peckett 1990 of 1940) shunts oil tanks for the A station, whose chimneys can be seen behind the line of trees; 11 June 1976.

were used occasionally, for example for weighbridge testing, before they were disposed of.

Three Peckett 0–4–0 saddle tanks were supplied new: no. 1 (works no. 1803) in 1933; no. 2 (1893) in 1936; and no. 3 (1990) in 1940. 1 and 3 worked at Ironbridge throughout their industrial careers; no. 2 left in 1951 to go to Birchills Power Station at Walsall, later moving back to the Severn Valley at Stourport Power Station. A further locomotive, *Anne*, a Bagnall (2828) of 1945, came to Ironbridge from Meaford, Staffordshire, in 1964. Nos. 1 and 3 both required overhaul at that time, so *Anne* was able to deputize, but she was little used afterwards and was sold for scrap in 1969. The two Pecketts both left Ironbridge in 1980; no. 1 went to the Foxfield Railway in Staffordshire, where it remains,

and no. 3 ended up at Horsehay. Neither of them is currently in working order. The other Peckett, no. 2, also lives on, at Coleford GWR in the Forest of Dean. Although restored to working order in 2005, it is mostly on static display.

BSC Allscott

The UK's first factory to produce sugar from sugar beet opened in Cantley, Norfolk, in 1912. Several others opened during the following years, until by the mid-1930s there were eighteen sugar factories in operation, owned by thirteen different companies. In 1936, the industry was brought under the control of the British Sugar Corporation, an organization in which the Government would be a major shareholder until the 1980s. The BSC would manage the entire UK sugar beet crop.

With a bulky raw material and the need for other materials, principally coal, it was natural that these factories were constructed close to railway lines. Transport of beet products (other than the sugar itself) by rail, at reduced freight charges, also entitled such installations to a reduction in their local authority rating assessments.

The factory at Allscott, beside the Shrewsbury line about 3 miles (5km) west of Wellington, was opened in 1927 by the Shropshire Beet Sugar Company. To work the extensive sidings, an 0–6–0 saddle tank *Lewisham* was obtained from Bagnall of Stafford (works no. 2221 of 1927). It was joined in 1928 by a second-hand locomotive *Yorkshire*,

Industrial steam and main-line diesel at Ironbridge Power Station, June 1979. Although one or two duties could be found for the Ironbridge Pecketts, they were effectively redundant once the A station had closed in 1978. Both left for preservation during 1980.

a 1914-built Hudswell Clarke (no. 1070), which remained at Allscott until 1951, when it left to work at the Ipswich factory. *Yorkshire* was replaced by a new Ruston and Hornsby diesel, 304474 of 1951, and another diesel arrived in October 1969, an ex-BR 0–6–0 no. D2302. With two diesels on site, *Lewisham* was effectively redundant, but like so many of Shropshire's industrial locomotives, it avoided the scrapyard and since 1970 it has been preserved at the Foxfield Railway in Staffordshire.

By the early 1980s, use of the internal railway at Allscott had ended. Materials were now arriving by road and the diesels were disposed of. After a number of moves, D2302 ended up at Moreton Park in Herefordshire, where it lives in the company of two other ex-BR shunters, the property of the D2578 Locomotive Group. The Ruston diesel was scrapped in late 1983.

The Allscott factory closed in 2007 and the site has been cleared. UK sugar beet processing is now concentrated on just four major works, all in eastern England. Residents of Wellington knew when the 'campaign' had commenced – each year, shortly after processing of that season's harvest had begun, a distinctive sweet aroma would be carried on the prevailing westerly winds. Like the factory, the aroma is now just a local memory.

GKN Sankey

The Hadley Castle works in northern Telford has been a major local employer for many years and has an interesting history. Industrial use of the site dates back to the late nineteenth century, when an ironworks was established by Nettlefold and Chamberlain. Several changes of use and ownership led eventually to the works being owned by Joseph Sankey in 1911. Within ten years it was part of the Guest, Keen & Nettlefolds (GKN) empire,

Portrait of industrial steam – the everyday grimy working locomotive that preservation cannot recreate. Lewisham (Bagnall 2221 of 1927) spent its working life at Allscott sugar works. Seen in 1969, it left Allscott the following year for its new home at Foxfield, where it has remained. ROB WESTON

though locals still refer to 'Sankey's'. The Guest family came from Broseley, Shropshire, where the county's first rails were laid.

For a time the works was part of the Birkenhead firm of G.F. Milnes, turning out around 1,600 tramcars over a short period at the start of the twentieth century. At least two of its products, trailers nos 42 and 43, survive on the Manx Electric Railway, but Milnes failed. The works closed in 1904, to be revived within a year and operated by Metropolitan Amalgamated, which produced railway carriages and wagons for about three years. Closed again,

Lewisham is hard at work with a rake of coal wagons in the sugar factory sidings. ROB WESTON

the factory was 'mothballed' until Joseph Sankey came along. Output has since been varied, increasingly focused on automotive products as the years went by. During the war, 868 Spitfires were built at Hadley, plus armoured vehicles were produced there until relatively recently, though that part of the business was sold to Alvis in 1998.

The works was rail-connected from early days, the sidings shunted by locomotives of the main-line company – admittedly, they were of similar size to the smaller industrials. The LMS used former Caledonian 'Pugs', 16004 and 16027, for several years and later an ex-L&YR locomotive, 11218, was used. During World War II, a Peckett 0–4–0ST was borrowed from the Lilleshall Company, to be displaced after a short period by a pair of Fowler diesels. In 1957, a more powerful diesel was obtained, North British no. 27414 of 1954, and later the Fowlers were displaced by a Hudswell Clarke from GKN's Cwmbran plant, D843 of 1954.

Rail traffic into the Hadley works ended in 1972; four years later, both surviving locomotives were sold into preservation. The North British locomotive is now at Horsehay and the Hudswell Clarke at Oswestry.

Ministry of Defence, Donnington

The MoD's use of railways in the county has already been noted. The Donnington, northern Telford, facility also dates from World War II, but, unlike the others, continues to function. Resulting from the decision, when the war loomed, to move Army Ordnance Stores away from vulnerable Woolwich, it was located beside the former Wellington to Stafford line, where it could be served by both the GWR and the LMS systems.

Donnington operated an internal railway with a network of tracks, connected to an internal East Yard and the main exchange sidings/yard at Trench. The yards were capable of holding up to 700 wagons. From the establishment of the depot until the end of steam in the early 1960s, as many as six locomotives might be seen working. Almost all were 0–6–0 Austerity saddle tanks, from a variety of manufacturers. Some were delivered new to Donnington, some came from other MoD sites, or from service elsewhere during the war. At least twenty-three are known to have spent some time there, though some would be resident only for storage purposes. Two US-built 0–6–0 tanks, dating from 1943, can be included, but Army secrecy being what it is, all that is known about the 'foreigners' is that they were there, at some time.

Steam was displaced by three new Ruston and Hornsby diesels in 1961–2. Like the steam fleet, these and other diesels came and went; when use of the internal railway ended in 1991, the last three locomotives, nos 420, 427 and 432, were of the same kind as the first three. Only no. 432 was still in working order, though all appeared immaculate. There were also two Hunslet 2ft 0in (610mm) gauge diesels on site from 1940 until the mid-1950s. Given the vast scale of the stores, it is possible that they were, in effect, forgotten …

The last day of the MoD's internal railway at Donnington: Ruston and Hornsby diesel no. 432 shunts a couple of internal user wagons in the exchange sidings, the site of today's new freight terminal. Behind can be seen construction work at Telford's Hortonwood industrial estate; 26 April 1991.

The incline was still in use on 26 June 1955, when these two photographs were taken. Looking down from the top, the three rails on the upper section ended at the halfway passing loop. *D.J. NORTON*

Clee Hill

The Ludlow and Clee Hill Railway and its associated connections are difficult to categorize. The railway, purely a mineral line, ran from Clee Hill Junction, Ludlow, to quarries at Dhustone, high on Titterstone Clee Hill. Shropshire's third highest hill, at 1,749ft (533m), has the curious distinction of being the only hill in England shown, by name, on the Mappa Mundi in Hereford cathedral, and derives its name from a large rocking stone that may once have existed high on its slopes. Dhustone is a hard black ('dhu') volcanic rock, a basalt well suited to road-making and similar purposes.

Initially independent, the railway opened in 1864 and became part of the GWR/LNWR joint network from 1893. It remained part of the national network until closure in 1962, but its operation was quite unlike other parts of the network. The quarries are around 5 miles (8km) from Ludlow and about 1,000ft (300m) higher. The line was reasonably straightforward as far as Middleton Siding, but then climbed steeply, with a final stretch at 1 in 20, to a yard at Bitterley.

Here locomotive haulage gave way to cable. An incline of 1¼ miles (2km) lifted the standard-gauge railway 600ft (180m) higher. Its gradient began at 1 in 12, steepening to 1 in 6 near the summit. A stationary steam engine at the top powered the cable, though it was effectively self-acting, as loaded wagons descending would pull up the empties.

There are two of these wagons, both attached to the cable. This one is at the top, the other is at the foot of the incline at Bitterley.
D.J. NORTON

The railway then extended a further 1¼ miles (2km) to the quarry screens. Although operated by the railway companies, it was to all intents and purposes a typical industrial railway (it is listed as such by the Industrial Railway Society in their book *Industrial Locomotives of Cheshire, Shropshire and Herefordshire*). Its locomotives were all four-wheeled and, because of the obvious difficulties, remained on the quarry-level railway for many years. In pre-grouping days, an LNWR

LMS Sentinel no. 7184, built 1928, at Clee Hill in the company of a number of British Quarrying Company wagons. Behind are tipper wagons on the 3ft 0in gauge quarry internal lines. SELWYN PEARCE HIGGINS

Ramsbottom 0–4–0 saddle tank was used (no. 3266, built 1892). Later residents included LMS (and, for a while, LNER) Sentinels, although ex-Lancashire and Yorkshire and Caledonian 'Pugs' (nos 11221 and 16027) were tried briefly. The last of the Sentinels was replaced by an ex-Swansea Harbour Trust 0–4–0 saddle tank, no. 1142, in July 1957. Withdrawn in 1959, it was replaced by its twin, no. 1143, which lasted until the end of working above the incline.

Road traffic had been slowly but surely replacing rail for a number of years and the incline was seeing little use by the end of the 1950s. When in 1960 the track was found to have been vandalized, the railway above Bitterley closed. The *Railway Magazine* records that no. 1143 went for scrap on 14 November of that year, the incline being specially opened in order to take it down on its final journey.

Some rail-borne traffic remained, stone being taken by road from the quarry to Bitterley yard and trans-shipped there until October 1962. The remains of the branch to Ludlow were closed at the end of that year.

The Clee Hill Quarry Co. had its own standard gauge shunter for some years – unusually, an American-built locomotive, a Baldwin (works no. 43201 of 1916), which it bought from the ROD. It was used until the quarry was taken over by the British Quarrying Company. For a while, a steam crane was used to shunt, but later the BR locomotive performed the work. For a time, there were 3ft 0in (914mm) gauge railways within the quarries, displaced by dumpers from 1929.

The quarries and railways described so far were on the southern part of Titterstone Clee, sometimes described as 'Clee Hill'. Titterstone Clee proper

3ft 0in gauge Avonside 1666 was new to the Titterstone Clee Quarry in 1913 and bore the name Titterstone – unusually, across the back of the cab. Its working life was over when this photograph was taken in December 1951 – use of locomotives at the quarries ended that year and Titterstone was scrapped a couple of years later. KEN COOPER PHOTOGRAPH, COPYRIGHT INDUSTRIAL RAILWAY SOCIETY

forms the more northerly part of this upland area and had its own quarries and railway. Originally operated by Messrs Field and Mackay, these quarries became the property of the British Quarrying Company in 1929. Stone from the quarry faces was conveyed on a 3ft 0in gauge railway to the crusher, from which point a second incline, also 3ft 0in gauge, descended to Bitterley yard for transshipment. To work the quarry level, a second-hand Bagnall 0–4–0 saddle tank (1717 of 1903) had been acquired in 1910 and a new Avonside 0–4–0 side tank (1666) was obtained in 1913. In 1926, a new Sentinel locomotive (6222) joined the fleet. The Bagnall went for scrap around 1940; when road vehicles replaced the railway in 1952, the track was lifted and the remaining locomotives also went for scrap.

Quarrying continues at Clee Hill, though the Titterstone quarries have long since closed. A road (signed 'Dhustone') leaves the Ludlow to Cleobury Mortimer road high on the slopes of Clee Hill and can be followed (crossing the top of the former standard-gauge incline) to the old Titterstone workings. Many derelict concrete structures remain around the quarry level, where there is space to park and explore. The remainder of the road (private from this point) can be walked to the radar station and on past its curious mushroom-like structures to the summit itself. The views are extensive – and the trackbeds of the two inclines can clearly be seen descending towards Bitterley, a distinctive reminder of the industrial past of these hills.

Narrow-Gauge Lines

Although steam was used widely on the narrow gauge, the classic twentieth-century industrial narrow-gauge railway used internal-combustion locomotives. Several manufacturers built large numbers of locomotives; some of the best known were: Motor Rail (Bedford); Lister (Dursley); Ruston and Hornsby (Lincoln); Hibberd (Park Royal) and Hunslet (Leeds). Lister built very light locomotives, often used in peat extraction. Motor

Rail's product, the Simplex, originated in designs for the World War I trenches and was again of relatively light construction. Hunslet narrow-gauge locomotives were often handled by Hudson of Leeds, which was a well-known supplier of narrow-gauge railway equipment.

Some of the earlier examples used petrol engines, while others were described as 'petrol or paraffin', using petrol to start, then switching to the cheaper fuel once warmed up. Diesels ultimately proved to be more robust, reliable and economical.

Llanforda Hall

Perhaps the best-known industrial narrow-gauge railway in the county – certainly the last to operate – was at Llanforda Hall near Oswestry, home of the Liverpool Corporation Waterworks (later North West Water Authority) filter beds. Water from their reservoir, Lake Vyrnwy, is passed through beds of sand, which requires washing and replacing at regular intervals. To handle the sand, a 2ft 0in (610mm) gauge railway was used. Over the years, a variety of locomotives operated here, including several Rustons, two Hudson Hunslets and a Hibberd. Locomotives would sometimes move between Oswestry and a similar facility at Rivington in Lancashire.

A Hunslet diesel (6299 of 1964) shunts v-skips of sand from the filter beds on the 2ft 0in gauge system at Llanforda Hall, near Oswestry, on 24 October 1980.

When the author visited the site in October 1980, a Ruston and a Hunslet were in use, but three other locomotives were also on site. Rail operations ceased some six years later and, happily, several of the locomotives have survived. Two of the Rustons are now owned by the Cambrian Railways Society, along with one of the Hunslets; the other Hunslet and the Hibberd are now at the Moseley Railway Trust's Apedale Valley Railway, near Newcastle-under-Lyme in Staffordshire.

Westbury Brick and Pipe Co.

Immediately north of Westbury station, on the Shrewsbury to Welshpool line, was the Sarn Brick and Tile Works belonging to the Westbury Brick and Pipe Co. When the station closed in 1960, the works was still using a 2ft 0in (610mm) gauge railway, similar to many other such businesses around the country, wherever suitable clay deposits are found. The railway brought clay to the works from pits about a quarter of a mile (400m) away, until the pits closed in 1963, clay then being brought in from elsewhere. The business was also served by a standard-gauge siding.

The railway continued to see some use around the works until 1971. In its earlier days, the company had used a 1933 Ruston and Hornsby diesel and a 1935 Lister petrol locomotive; both were scrapped in 1958, replaced by a Motor Rail diesel. Another Motor Rail followed in 1962 and was bought for preservation in 1972.

Basalts Ltd

Basalts had quarries at Doseley, near Horsehay, and at Lawrence Hill, near Wellington. A substantial fleet of locomotives was used, mostly at Doseley; of those that can be identified precisely, most were built by Hibberd and Motor Rail in the 1920s and 1930s, but unusually two German-built locomotives were also in use. The railways were displaced by road vehicles in the 1950s and the locomotives went, mostly for scrap, in the late 1950s and early 1960s. Once again, there remains a survivor – a Motor Rail, which is preserved at the Bromyard & Linton Light

Railway, Herefordshire, in the company, *inter alia*, of the locomotive from Westbury.

Blockleys Ltd

Blockleys still makes bricks and pavers in its modern brickworks at Hadley, Telford. The works was formerly connected to its nearby clay pit by a 2ft 0in (610mm) gauge railway, which also connected to the nearby Coalport branch line.

Brown Clee

The Abdon Clee Quarrying Company used 2ft 0in (610mm) gauge lines within the quarries. Operated at first by horses, the inevitable ex-War Department Motor Rail petrol tractors arrived in 1918 (nos 848 and 1029, both built the same year). The quarrymen called them 'whizz-bangs'.

Cothercott Mining Co.

Cothercott Mining, in the hills above Pulverbatch, used a steam locomotive. *Minstrel Park*, originally *George*, was one of the first locomotives to be built for the North Wales slate industry, in 1877 (Hunslet works no. 184). Relatively old and non-standard by the early twentieth century, it was sold and found its way to Shropshire. It was used to haul barytes from adits on the northern side of Cothercott Hill to the dressing mill beside the road. The mine closed in 1928; *Minstrel Park* survived for another fourteen years before being scrapped around 1942.

Donnington Wood Brickworks

On the smallest railways, individual wagons could be moved by human effort, sometimes in conjunction with rope or chain haulage, as at Donnington Wood Brickworks, part of the Lilleshall Company's empire in east Shropshire. An endless chain moved wagons to and fro along an 18in (457mm) gauge plateway, the chain being dropped into, and lifted out of, a slotted plate at one end of the wagons. The wagons were manhandled as required at either end of their journey. The line is thought to have begun operation in this manner some time after World War I, continuing in use until 1971.

CHAPTER 7

Preservation, Leisure and Heritage

Beginnings

Shropshire's best-known heritage railway – the Severn Valley – has been in operation since 1970, when railway preservation was in its infancy. However, preservation of railway artefacts in the county had begun some years earlier, under the aegis of the Ironbridge Gorge Museum Trust and its predecessors.

No. 5, an 0–4–0 saddle tank, was built at Coalbrookdale around 1865 for service at the works, where it operated until 1932; it was then sold to Bardon Hill Quarries (Ellis and Everard Ltd), seeing service there until 1956. Brought back to Coalbrookdale in October 1959, it is now displayed at the Enginuity Museum in Coalbrookdale. Cosmetically restored, no. 5 can be moved (slightly!) by visitors as part of a hands-on display demonstrating the use of pulleys.

The remains of two other locomotives are preserved at the Coalbrookdale site. They are 1925 rebuilds by Sentinel, with vertical boiler and

Early days at Coalbrookdale: no. 5 stands in the open air a few yards from Darby's 'coke hearth', as it is still known locally, in May 1970. It is now indoors, cosmetically restored, at the nearby interactive Enginuity, one of the ten Ironbridge Gorge Museums.

Also seen the same day at Blists Hill is this newly installed 2´0″ gauge line – the 'Clay Mine Railway' takes visitors into a mock-up mine to view an audio-visual presentation. The push-pull train is powered by a small battery locomotive Sir Peter Gadsden, built by Alan Keef Ltd (no. 84) in 2008.

vertical cylinders, of conventional locomotives, an 1873 Manning Wardle and Coalbrookdale no. 6, built shortly after no. 5 above.

Peter, the Andrew Barclay 0–6–0ST (782 of 1896) originally supplied to Kinlet Colliery, is on display at Blists Hill, cosmetically restored. It returned to Shropshire in September 1969, from its last employment at Lunt, Comley, Pitt Ltd at Shut End, Staffordshire.

Also at Blists Hill are some active exhibits, which are not truly 'preserved'. The 1990-built replica of Trevithick's – and the world's – first steam railway locomotive, built at Coalbrookdale in 1802, is operated from time to time. Built to run on a 3ft 0in (914mm) gauge plateway, its single cylinder powers a large flywheel, which connects to the wheels by a series of gears. Unusual among steam locomotives, it sometimes needs to be 'bump-started' by hand-rotating the flywheel and is capable, by disconnecting the gears, of 'ticking over'.

A 2ft 0in (610mm) gauge railway opened in 2009. The battery-powered electric locomotive and its tiny four-wheeled carriages, supplied by Alan Keef Ltd, are finished in a smart plain green livery. The locomotive and the driving trailer bear the nameplates *Sir Peter Gadsden* – he was chairman of the museum trust until his death in 2006. The train runs into the clay mine exhibit, where museum visitors are shown an audio/visual 'mine experience' presentation.

The Incline Plane Lift, opened at the same time, is a distant relation of the Bridgnorth Cliff Railway – though mechanically it is more closely related to the funicular railway installed at Le Tréport, France, in 2006. A single car, user-operated (like a conventional lift), runs with unflanged wheels on plain rails, with a separate rail and horizontal wheels for guidance.

Bridgnorth's inland Cliff Railway is no longer the only one in Shropshire – though whether this one is truly a railway is debatable. At the Blists Hill Victorian Town, it is described as an 'Incline Lift'; 25 August 2009.

The Severn Valley Railway

The Severn Valley Railway (SVR) was not the first preserved railway. The narrow-gauge Talyllyn Railway got there some nineteen years earlier, in 1951, while the standard-gauge Bluebell Railway in Sussex and the Middleton Railway near Leeds both began operating in preservation in 1960. Nevertheless, when services began between Bridgnorth and Hampton Loade in 1970, it was one of a mere handful. At 16 miles (26km), it is not the longest – the West Somerset and North Yorkshire Moors railways are both longer. It does not quite achieve the latter's passenger numbers either – though around a quarter of a million per year makes it a very substantial tourist attraction. Without doubt, the Severn Valley Railway is one of Britain's top 'heritage railways'.

After the through route from Bewdley to Shrewsbury closed in 1963, the track between Bridgnorth and Buildwas was lifted, but remained in place southwards to Bewdley. Coal trains continued to run from Alveley Colliery sidings until closure in 1969. Further south, in Worcestershire, passenger trains still ran from Bewdley to Kidderminster (now the southernmost part of the SVR), and to Hartlebury Junction (the original route, now closed and lifted).

Preservation attempts began in 1965; early fundraising efforts were sufficiently successful to persuade BR not to lift the track. Within a couple of years, the first locomotives and rolling stock had begun to arrive. In common with other early preserved railways, the SVR was fortunate in being able to obtain its first locomotives direct from BR, complete and more or less in working order. Steam-operated public services along the 4½ miles (7km) to Hampton Loade commenced on 23 May 1970.

Running trains generates income and the SVR was soon able to pay the balance of the purchase price of the 5-mile (8km) stretch to Alveley Colliery sidings, now no longer in use. The end of the BR Bewdley to Hartlebury and Kidderminster service at the beginning of 1970 had already set the stage for expansion.

The first part of that expansion followed just four years after the opening trains. In April 1974, trains ran to Highley and a month later (crossing now into Worcestershire) through Arley to Bewdley – 12½ miles (20km) from Bridgnorth. It would be another ten years before the last section, a little over 3 miles (5km) to Kidderminster, opened. Until 1982, the final mile remained in BR use, serving Kidderminster sugar factory.

The Severn Valley is now home to around twenty former main-line steam locomotives. More than half are of GWR design and most of the remainder are ex-LMS. Several are sole survivors of their type, such as the Ivatt Class 4 2-6-0 no. 43106 and Stanier 2-6-0 no. 42968. Similarly, GWR 15XX pannier tank no. 1501 and Port Talbot Railway 0-6-0ST no. 813 are the only representatives of

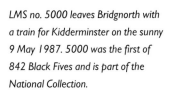
LMS no. 5000 leaves Bridgnorth with a train for Kidderminster on the sunny 9 May 1987. 5000 was the first of 842 Black Fives and is part of the National Collection.

Ex-GWR pannier tank 5764 hauls a demonstration freight train past the crossing at Eardington during the September 1995 Steam Gala.

BELOW: No. 193, ex-Shropshire and Montgomeryshire (MoD) Austerity 0-6-0 saddle tank, is hard at work on the Severn Valley's Eardington bank on 15 April 1978. Later the same day, it was formally named Shropshire. Not best suited to heavy trains on a relatively long line, it has since left the railway.

their classes, as was class 2251 no 3205, which has since left the railway.

Disaster struck the Severn Valley Railway in 2007. On the evening of 19 June, a severe thunderstorm and torrential rain caused major damage in the area, including to the railway's infrastructure. A lengthy section of the surface of the only road into Hampton Loade was washed away, barely significant when the railway is considered. A section of embankment nearby was washed into the caravan park below, leaving the rails suspended. At Highley, a 75yd (69m) section of embankment was swept away. Similar damage occurred along the whole section between Bridgnorth and Bewdley. The Bewdley to Kidderminster line was unaffected.

Further heavy rain on 24 June compounded existing damage, so that by 26 June, the total number of significantly damaged locations totalled around forty-five. This had been the worst natural disaster to date to strike a preserved railway.

If such a disaster had struck in the railway's formative years, the Severn Valley Railway as we know it would almost certainly not exist. It is a measure of the status of the line, in terms of tourism, the local economy and the heritage railway movement generally, to record that the railway reopened in full the following Easter, at a total cost of around £3.7m. Of that total, a public appeal raised more

The Severn Valley Railway doing what it excels at – visiting LNER A4 Pacific no. 4464 Bittern hauls eight LNER teak coaches near Eardington, recreating a scene from the 1930s at the March 2012 Steam Gala.

than £500,000, but by far the biggest part came from the Heritage Lottery Fund and European Regional Development Fund.

In June 2012, the SVR was awarded the English Tourist Board's bronze medal in the 'Tourism Experience of the Year' category – reinforcing the railway's national status beyond the field of railway preservation.

From time to time, suggestions and proposals pop up relating to the route of the railway north of Bridgnorth, via Linley and Coalport to Ironbridge. Immediately north of the tunnel under Bridgnorth town centre, houses have been built on the trackbed. Beyond lies Bridgnorth Golf Club – the former trackbed now difficult to trace through the fairways. Northwards again, it serves as a means of

access to scattered farms and houses in this part of the valley. Near Jackfield, the ground is extremely unstable. A major landslip in 1952 caused, over the course of several days, many houses to collapse and slide into the river. The railway was only kept open by the daily efforts of the gangers. In 1984, two public houses and numerous dwellings were cut off when a stretch of the only road slipped into the river. Access was reinstated using the railway trackbed; a wooden slatted section remains to this day. Immediately beyond, the road, still on the former railway, dips and winds alarmingly. Perhaps unsurprisingly, the official SVR view, stated on its website, is that 'there is now no possibility of Severn Valley trains reaching Ironbridge and Shrewsbury ever again'.

In common with other similar heritage railways, several of the Severn Valley's steam locomotives have been restored to working order, but have since retired in need of overhaul and repair. Unlike other railways, the SVR is fortunate in now being able to keep them under cover in its Engine House Museum at Highley – providing an extra attraction for visitors and reducing the amount of cosmetic restoration needed when the locomotives are eventually overhauled. No. 600 Gordon is in such a situation; the Midland Railway's compound no. 1000 is on loan from the National Railway Museum; 31 May 2008.

SHROPSHIRE RAILWAYMEN – JAMIE GREEN

Jamie Green is a volunteer signalman on the Severn Valley Railway. A recent graduate of Aberystwyth University, he read history before taking his master's degree in Heritage Skills; his dissertation subject was 'Visitor Expectations when visiting Heritage Railways'. He commented that many will pontificate, but no one appeared to have made an objective study of the subject.

Many steam railway enthusiasts are inevitably 'of an age', given that main-line steam ended in 1968. Yet steam trains were a part of Jamie's childhood – the preserved variety, on the Severn Valley Railway. He talks of frequent visits with his grandparents to Bridgnorth and Highley, as well as picnics against a backdrop of passing steam. His father was a volunteer on the Bala Lake Railway in Wales, where Jamie has also spent some time – 'a few firing turns'. Semaphore signalling was an early influence too – a friend of his grandfather worked the box at Highley, where during a number of visits Jamie would sit, listen, watch and soak up the atmosphere.

The author and Jamie talked through his SVR role one afternoon while he was operating Bewdley South box: 'It's more like a main-line box than others on the SVR – it's neither on nor beside the platform.' There were no single-line tokens (see below) to collect nor hand over either, unlike boxes further north. Discussions were interrupted (quite properly) from time to time while train movements were dealt with. GWR 2–8–0 no. 2857, 7812 *Erlestoke Manor*, Bulleid Pacific 34053 *Sir Keith Park* and diesel D1062 *Western Courier* rumbled past. Jamie commented: 'It could be all be automated, of course, but … ' Visitor expectations need to be taken in to account. The bell codes rang out from time to time – ting-ting-ting, ting for an ordinary passenger train. Passengers waved as Jamie leant out to see the trains pass. No, it could not be automated, could it?

Jamie joined the SVR with the intention of working as a volunteer, starting on 'platform' duties at Arley in 2000: 'Yes, a bit like the old 'porter', and yes, there's plenty of lifting – all those buggies. There are hundreds of them when the Santa trains are running.' The signalling course in January 2010 was successfully completed by written exam in June ('it's a 75 per cent pass mark'). In May the following year, Jamie passed for Hampton Loade and, just over a year later, Bridgnorth. The responsibility weighed heavily at first, he explained, but briefly – he quickly settled into the routine.

Experiences of Hampton Loade and Bridgnorth boxes and their similarities and differences are compared. Hampton Loade has a nicely authentic feel, being a pleasantly quiet branch-line station, with views from the box to the river. There is also the need to be outdoors frequently, in all weathers, for the single-line tokens. Bridgnorth box faces, and is downwind of, the locomotive shed, which makes it a dusty box. It is also busier. Locomotives have to run round their trains, or may have to go on and off shed, and there may be a shunt to signal. It is less isolated than Hampton Loade – there are plenty of other members of the railway staff around. A guard will often come into the box for a break between trains. Jamie emphasized the social aspects of volunteering, explaining that perhaps 25 per cent of volunteers are under thirty and a degree of socializing takes place outside the railway.

Those of us 'of an age' have much gratitude to this new generation of railwaymen and women, who will be running the heritage railways, we hope, when our generation is no longer capable.

They were a common sight on the Severn Valley line in latter days: GWR railcar no. 22, dating from 1940, was resident at Bridgnorth in the early years of preservation, later moving to the Great Western Society at Didcot. It is seen here at Bridgnorth on a return visit in May 1990.

The Telford Steam Railway

In the last years of the rail connection to Horsehay works, the Telford Development Corporation (TDC) had designated Spring Village – the area around Horsehay Pool, including the works' disued loco shed – as a conservation area. Ownership of the pool and the shed would transfer to TDC. Perhaps

an appropriate locomotive should occupy the shed? Through the Ironbridge Gorge Museum Trust, TDC arranged the purchase of ex-GWR 56XX class 0–6–2T no 5619 from Dai Woodham's scrapyard at Barry. The Telford Horsehay Steam Trust (THST), which came into being on 1 March 1976, developed from the working party established to organize the purchase. The shed itself is of some historical

It is very nearly the end of BR freight specials on the Lightmoor to Horsehay line. 25009 slowly draws two substantial pieces of structural steelwork out of the works on 30 April 1979. Behind the locomotive is BR 08019, which is assisting with the various reversals required. Also in the scene are an ex-GWR autocoach and the North British diesel from GKN Sankey, in the care of the Telford Horsehay Steam Trust. PHIL DARLASTON

significance, having been built for trans-shipment of goods between the local plateway system and the main line.

It was still relatively early days for the Steam Trust when the Horsehay branch, as it was by then, closed and the Trust was unable to prevent the lifting of most of the track down to Lightmoor Junction. Nevertheless, rapid progress was made on no. 5619, which was successfully steamed in 1981. Other locomotives began to gather, in customary fashion, though most moved on to other railways. One that stayed, seeing some service at Horsehay, is the former Ironbridge Power Station Peckett, no. 3. The ex-LNWR 'Super D' 0-8-0, BR no. 49395, spent some time here undergoing cosmetic restoration, as

did the Coalbrookdale 0-4-0ST no. 5 and Blists Hill's *Peter*.

The line opened to passengers in 1981 – although there was precious little line to operate on! Trains started from a platform near the loco shed – now known as 'Spring Village' – and were propelled out of the yard on to the former main line. They would then reverse down to the former Horsehay and Dawley station, before returning in similar fashion.

Some thirty-odd years later, the train service still operates in this way, although more of the main line northwards, towards Heath Hill tunnel, is available for locomotives to 'stretch their legs' a little. But track now extends through the tunnel to Lawley Common, where a new platform and run-round

Ex-GWR 0-6-2T no. 5619 has been restored to working order – locomotive and driver pause for thought at Horsehay on 29 July 1984. Behind the locomotive stands Horsehay works; since closed and demolished, the site is now occupied by housing and light industrial units.

Brighton 'Terrier' no. 662 Martello is guest of honour at a Telford Steam Railway Gala weekend, and is seen with a minimalist freight train at Horsehay and Dawley station on 28 May 2007.

from use elsewhere, has already been purchased, for installation when the time comes. Perhaps it is a pipe dream – but a steam railway carrying visitors through Coalbrookdale (with a fine aerial view of the historic works from the curving viaduct), to a station within yards of the world's first iron bridge, would surely be a winner?

The Cambrian Railways

The last passenger trains on the former Cambrian Railways main line from Buttington Junction to Whitchurch ran in January 1965; the shuttle along the former GWR link to Gobowen lingered on until November the following year. However, stone traffic continued to flow from the quarries around Porthywaen, through Oswestry, to the main line at Gobowen. The remainder of the track was lifted. The railway works at Oswestry, the biggest local employer, closed in 1966, but its buildings remain – as does the main station building. The plural in the old company's title 'The Cambrian Railways' is reflected in the preservation schemes involving its lines.

The Cambrian Railways Society

Local enthusiasts and former railwaymen set up the Cambrian Railways Society in Oswestry in 1972, establishing a small exhibits museum and assembling a collection of ex-industrial steam and diesel

loop should soon be completed. Once this extension is open, the next moves will be southwards. Track has been laid for about three-quarters of a mile (1.2km), but beyond this point lie major expansion plans for the medium to long term.

Ironbridge Power Station is due to close by the end of 2015. The railway route down through Coalbrookdale could then be available to the Telford Steam Railway. The railway's stated 'ultimate aim' is to provide a journey by steam from Lawley Common to Buildwas. Perhaps when the cooling towers have gone, engines could reverse and run along the former Severn Valley line, running high above the Severn on that curious half-viaduct, to Ironbridge itself. A major obstacle is the severed trackbed where it crosses the Ironbridge bypass. However, a suitable bridge structure, redundant

The short-lived Telford Town Tramway's locomotive was named Thomas by the Rev. W. Awdry on 9 April 1980. It moved to Horsehay in the mid-1980s and is regularly steamed there on its 2ft 0in (610mm) gauge track behind the loco shed.

locomotives. The latter operated from time to time at open days and similar events, on the sidings between the goods shed (housing the museum) and the station, but there was no railway on which passenger services could run. Without the cash flow that passenger fares would generate, scope for raising much-needed funds was limited and little progress was possible. Since the late 1980s, with a subsequent Light Railway Order in 1995, the Society has had the use of a long siding beside the former main line, where brake-van shuttles can operate. Very recently, following renovation of the station building, the platform has been reinstated and is in use by the Society, providing a longer run for the ride.

In 1988, the last stone train ran on the British Rail line from the quarries to Gobowen and the line was 'mothballed'. The possibility of access to the Gobowen–Porthywaen railway (around 8½ miles [14km]) now presented itself – but so did a number of complications. In 1987, the A5/A483 Whittington bypass had virtually severed the line between Oswestry and Gobowen. With railway traffic by now very infrequent, probably moribund, the bypass was constructed to cross the line on the level. While traffic on the very busy road could perhaps be stopped occasionally for a freight train, it seems unlikely that this could be allowed several times a day for a heritage railway service.

A further complication followed with the privatization of British Rail on 1 April 1994. A new private body, Railtrack, was now responsible for the line. Railtrack collapsed in the aftermath of the October 2000 Hatfield crash, to be replaced by Network Rail. It was not a good time for a small society trying to negotiate access to an almost forgotten stretch of line.

The Cambrian Railways Trust

The formation of the Cambrian Railways Trust in 1998 may, in part, be a consequence of those tricky times. Bringing in local authority and business representation, as well as some Cambrian Railways Society representation, it focused initially on the Gobowen–Porthywaen railway. Difficulties in discussions with the line's owners, as well as in

The Cambrian Heritage Railways preservationists at Oswestry have recently resurfaced the platform and replaced a signal at the former Cambrian HQ. Diesel Telemon is working the brake-van shuttle to Middleton Road Bridge. In the right background the former railway works can be seen; 14 April 2013.

This delightful little country station at Llynclys has been built by the preservationists at the north end of the relaid section (to Pen-y-garreg Lane, Pant) of the former main line; 19 February 2013.

the relationship with the Society, led to a change of focus to the long-abandoned trackbed south of Llynclys station. Within a few years, a line of rails had been laid along approximately 1,200yd (1,100m) of the old Cambrian main line, as far as Pant. In July 2005, the railway began carrying passengers, using former main-line diesel multiple units. An attractive small station has been constructed at Llynclys South and, more recently, a halt constructed at Pant.

Llynclys South is only a few yards away from the old Llynclys station, now a private dwelling whose garden occupies the trackbed. Connection to the dormant railway at Llynclys Junction, barely 400yd (370m) beyond, may not be easy. Similarly, an overbridge immediately beyond the southern terminus would need to be reinstated before track could be extended further in that direction.

Nantmawr – the Tanat Valley Light Railway

Around the same time as the reopening from Llynclys South, there were stirrings elsewhere. About 2 miles (3km) west from Llynclys, on the Tanat Valley road, a bridge crosses the Nantmawr branch, the remarkable short survivor of the ill-fated 'Potts'. The rails saw their last train in the early 1970s and nature gradually took over, until the route became, for much of its length, a linear forest. The author's visit in September 2004 confirmed that, despite sizable trees growing among

them, the rails had never been lifted. A group of Cambrian Railways Society members had acquired the branch during that summer and soon began clearing the vegetation. Now operating as the Tanat Valley Light Railway Company, they were able to offer rides on the top half a mile (800m) or so in November 2009, using the little ex-Gorton works shunter, Beyer Peacock 1827 of 1879, plus a former GWR 'Toad' brake van. Built and operated purely as a mineral line, these were the Nantmawr branch's first public passenger trains. With further track available to the north, rides are planned using an ex-BR DMU.

The Cambrian Heritage Railways

In 2008, the line from Gobowen to Llanddu, at the foot of the Nantmawr branch, was bought by Shropshire County Council and, the following year, renewed discussions between the Society and the Trust led to formal agreement to work together – effectively, to merge. It would seem that this is a sensible way to proceed – among the fragmented efforts at Oswestry, Llynclys and Nantmawr lies the scope and potential for a first-rate heritage railway. Most of the track is in place. If we consider pipe dreams again, most of the trackbed of the old 'Potts' is still intact between Llanymynech and Blodwell Junction. The (fairly serious) suggestion has been heard that this could be a long-term aim for reinstatement. The biggest 'balloon loop' in the heritage rail movement could make a unique attraction.

Nantmawr – the last short survivor of the 'Potts' has been cleared of trees and, on weekends in November 2009, tiny Beyer Peacock 1827 of 1879 steamed up and down part of the line with a GWR 'Toad' brake van – offering the first passenger service in the branch's history.

Market Drayton

The town famed for its gingerbread lost its last passenger service in September 1963 and, within a year, the A53 bypass was being discussed in Parliament. In a written answer, transport minister Ernest Marples said: 'Proposals for an interim scheme for by-passing the town have been put to me and the Market Drayton and District Road Safety Committee have asked that this scheme be carried out quickly.'

That bypass, constructed after freight ended in 1967, used part of the trackbed towards Wellington and severed the trackbed in the Nantwich direction, more or less at the junction with the North Staffordshire line. Nevertheless, in January 1992 the Market Drayton Railway Preservation Society came into being 'when the concept was launched to try to restore part or all of the former Nantwich to Market Drayton Railway as far north as Cox Bank on the outskirts of Audlem, about 4 miles of track'. Market Drayton station site was sold in 1994 and some of the material from the station was dismantled by the Society for possible future reuse. However, the Society has never reached the stage of acquiring track or rolling stock and the January 2010 name change to 'Nantwich & Market Drayton Railway Society' omits the word 'preservation', though the original aim continues to be stated on its website.

Other Schemes and a Museum

The War Department's last train ran on the S&M in February 1960 and within a couple of years the railway had been dismantled. However, part of the former depot at Kinnerley Junction proved suitable as a storage and restoration centre for the Welsh

A new use for old coaches: these former BR MkI coaches, now used as self-catering accommodation for tourists, stand at Coalport (GWR) station, on the former Severn Valley line; 11 April 2010.

Highland preservation group and, for a number of years, a variety of narrow-gauge (mostly 2ft 0in [610mm]) equipment was kept at the site, including *Russell*, the last surviving Welsh Highland locomotive built by Hunslet in 1906. The Welsh Highland Heritage Railway moved into its Gelert's Farm premises near Porthmadog in the mid-1970s and its locomotives soon joined them. Not all the locomotives at Kinnerley belonged to the Welsh Highland and some remained there for several more years.

A scheme to restore part or all of the Snailbeach District Railway was made public in 2006. Nothing tangible has come of this scheme, despite several years of claim and counter-claim.

More than fifty locomotives were gathered on a site near Cross Houses in the last years of the twentieth century. Known generally as the Shropshire Loco Collection, they were owned and stored by a

It is more than sixty years since Madeley Market's last passenger train stopped there, but it is still recognizably a railway station; 14 March 2013.

firm called Dealers. All of industrial origin, most were standard-gauge diesels, though there were a few steam locomotives and a small number of narrow-gauge battery locos. All have since been sold and have left the site; a small number, including the 0-4-0 crane tank *Glenfield*, built in 1902, and a 1950 Alco Bo-Bo diesel, stood for a few years outside McLarens antiques warehouse in Oswestry – the former Cambrian Railways works.

The Bishop's Castle Railway and Transport Museum is a collection of artefacts from the Bishop's Castle Railway, along with other railway and road transport items. BCR items range from tickets and paperwork to the fire irons used on 'Carlisle'; there is also a model railway depicting Lydham Heath station.

Main-Line Steam

BR's infamous '15 Guinea Special' ran on 11 August 1968, a week after the last regular steam trains. A steam ban was then declared across its network and it seemed that main-line steam had gone for ever. That ban was not quite complete, however – BR continued to operate the 2ft 0in (610mm) gauge Vale of Rheidol Railway and Alan Pegler, then owner of *Flying Scotsman*, had negotiated a contract with BR to be allowed to run on the main lines until 1972. Four more years perhaps? In the event, 4472 ran for one more year, before going to the United States, where it remained until 1973.

The first hint that the ban might not be permanent came in October 1971. A steam centre was being developed at H.P. Bulmer's cider factory in Hereford. Former GWR no. 6000, *King George V*, had arrived in 1968, followed by two ex-GWR pannier tanks and two former industrial steam locomotives. Peter Prior, then MD of Bulmer's, persuaded BR to allow a promotional run of the Bulmer 'Cider Train' – five Pullman coaches hauled by no. 6000. With additional coaches for fare-paying passengers, the train ran from Hereford to Tyseley, Birmingham, on 2 October. Two days later, it ran to London (Kensington Olympia), then returned to Hereford on 7 October.

Despite the elimination of much of the steam railway's infrastructure, such as coaling and watering facilities and turntables, there were no serious problems and the case was made for a limited 'Return to Steam' programme beginning in June 1972. Steam would only be allowed on certain lightly used routes, where operational steam locomotives were based nearby and where locomotives could be turned (on triangles) easily. The railway through the Welsh Marches was one such route and a year after no. 6000's ground-breaking trip, steam-hauled specials began to operate in the county.

Two more operational main-line locomotives arrived at Bulmer's in the following years – ex-LMS Pacific no. 6201 *Princess Elizabeth* and rebuilt Southern Railway Merchant Navy Pacific no. 35028 *Clan Line*. The trio became a regular, if not especially frequent, sight on the route from Newport to Chester, aided from time to time by other visitors.

Steam-hauled specials still run from time to time through the county, though less frequently

At the end of its career on BR, 60007 Sir Nigel Gresley was purchased for preservation. After refurbishment at Crewe, it made a number of running-in trips to Shrewsbury and is seen here at Coleham shed in the company of Class 24 diesels; Warship D843 Sharpshooter passes with a North and West freight; 30 July 1968. BERWYN STEVENS

LNER A3 no. 4472 Flying Scotsman has been in preservation since 1963 and was hauling rail tours before the end of steam on BR. It visited Shropshire in those early days and is seen here at Upton Magna with a special to Ruabon, running 'wrong line' while engineering work is carried out on the down main line; 9 May 1965. BERWYN STEVENS

LMS on the GWR: 5690 Leander storms up the bank towards Shifnal with the Severn Valley Limited on 2 October 2010. Leander hauled the train throughout from Bridgnorth to Blackpool and back.

Bearing a 'Cambrian Coast Express' headboard, 6024 King Edward I roars through Wellington's centre roads on 13 May 2006, recreating a scene from the early 1960s.

ABOVE: *Epitomizing North and West steam, 5029 Nunney Castle hauls 'The Great Britain IV' railtour south near All Stretton on 22 April 2011.*

LEFT: *Coalbrookdale saw its last steam-hauled passenger train in 1962; forty-five years later, GWR pannier tank 9466 worked a special down to Ironbridge Power Station, making quite a spectacle as it climbed back up the steep gradient; 3 November 2007.*

Main-line steam – new-build A1 Pacific no. 60163 Tornado crests the hump (exaggerated by the lens) in the track near Stokesay, south of Craven Arms, with the returning 'Cathedrals Express' on 12 May 2012.

than in the late 1970s and early 1980s. More routes became available for steam, and privatization and 'open access' led to the entire network (subject to engineering limitations such as loading gauge or weight) becoming available. All of Shropshire's passenger routes have seen steam operations in recent years, as has the freight-only line to Ironbridge Power Station. The number of onlookers, many of whom cannot remember everyday steam, continues to provide testimony to the attraction of the sight and sound of these runs.

Miniature Railways

The length of some miniature railways is measured in miles and they perform a useful transport role; at the other end of the range are models, often privately owned and operated, and outside the scope of this book. Within Shropshire, there are, or have been, a handful worth mentioning.

Lilleshall Abbey Woodland Railway

Shropshire's earliest pleasure railway opened in 1928, in the grounds of Lilleshall Hall, formerly the property of the Dukes of Sutherland. In 1927, ownership of the hall and gardens passed to a local man, Herbert Ford, who developed the estate with an eye to the leisure market. Its attractions included the gardens, putting and bowling greens, archery – and a 2ft 0in (610mm) gauge railway. Running from the hall towards the ruins of Lilleshall Abbey, it was described by the estate guide book as 'miniature'.

With a balloon loop at the Abbey end of the line, the total length of the ride was about 1¼ miles (2km). Rolling stock was provided by Baguley of Burton-on-Trent, which had developed a range of small petrol-engined locomotives. They had been designed for service on the World War I trench railways (internal combustion machines would not show a telltale plume of steam when operating). Their cylindrical water tanks, for cooling purposes, resembled steam locomotive boilers. Fitted with taller chimneys to further that impression, two such locomotives were purchased and set to work on the line. No. 1695 was delivered for the opening of the line; another, no. 1769, followed in 1929. Being more powerful, of enhanced appearance and, apparently, easier to start, it became the regular locomotive, with no. 1695 available when required.

The line closed at the outbreak of World War II; the locomotives were put into storage and the line lifted. In 1952, the newer locomotive and the coaches were bought for use at Alton Towers, where they saw service for more than forty years, by which time more sophisticated amusements had made them redundant. The locomotive was bought for preservation in 2002 and has since found its way, with two of the original coaches, to the Old Kiln Light Railway in Surrey. In the meantime, no. 1695 slumbered on until it was bought by the Rev. Teddy Boston in 1967 and taken to Cadeby. It now resides at the Apedale Valley Railway near Newcastle-under-Lyme, where it is in full working order, the only surviving such Baguley to retain its original 2-cylinder petrol engine.

This little petrol-engined Baguley was built in 1928 (works no. 1695) for the Lilleshall Abbey Woodland Railway. It is preserved in working order just outside the county, part of the Moseley Railway Trust's huge collection of narrow-gauge railway equipment at the Apedale Valley Railway near Newcastle-under-Lyme; 24 April 2010.

Hilton Valley Railway

Railways built to 2ft 0in (610mm) gauge are more usually 'narrow gauge' in purpose and appearance. Miniature railways are usually of smaller gauge and the 7¼in (184mm) gauge Hilton Valley was typical. It operated entirely within the grounds of Hilton House in the village of Hilton, on the Wolverhampton road from Bridgnorth. Michael Lloyd built the line in the 1960s, with a balloon-loop arrangement that was later extended to a second 'balloon'. The arrangement of loops and triangular junctions enabled operation with more than one train at once. Tokens for the single-line sections also operated the signals, by being hung on counterbalanced levers. With, ultimately, several steam locomotives available for use, a Sunday afternoon at Hilton could be very pleasant.

Sadly, following the death of the owner, the railway closed at the end of the 1979 season. Much of the equipment and rolling stock was used to create the miniature railway that operates at Weston Park, just outside the county boundary. The Weston Park line has since been developed with balloon loops at either end, providing a ride of around 1¼ miles (2km).

Woodseaves Miniature Railway

A relatively recent miniature railway exists near Market Drayton. Opened in 2003, the 7¼in (184mm) gauge Woodseaves Miniature Railway runs around a garden plants nursery and operates for the public on Sundays and bank holidays during the summer season. Its layout, roughly circular with a central link line (imagine an apple sliced through the centre) provides for a variety of routes. Trains are hauled by either a small steam locomotive, *Jean*, or a diesel, *Sydney*.

Canal Central Very Light Railway

A 10¼in (260mm) gauge line was constructed recently beside the Montgomery Canal near Maesbury Marsh. The Canal Central Very Light Railway was laid in the form of a 400yd (370m) circuit and has two locomotives, a steam 4–6–4 based on Canadian prototypes, as well as a small diesel. It operated for public passengers in September 2012, but does not yet operate regular services.

The Hilton Valley Railway: 7¼in gauge 4-8-2 Hilton Queen in action in the grounds of Hilton House, between Bridgnorth and Wolverhampton, in April 1973.

CHAPTER 8

Shropshire Railways Today

The Privatized Railway

On 1 April 1994, Britain's railways passed from the public sector to the private sector. Generally successful, 'sectorization' had been implemented from the 1980s onwards and would have some bearing on the nature of the privatization. Instead of geographically based structures, the railways were separated into business units. Railfreight, InterCity (the brand name had been in use for some years) and Provincial came into existence in 1982, with Network SouthEast following in 1986. Other than the London trains, Shropshire's passenger services fell under the Provincial banner. Scotrail would operate services within Scotland and various Passenger Transport Executives (PTEs) provided rail and road services in the metropolitan counties.

In 1991, a European Union directive required member states to separate 'the management of railway operation and infrastructure from the provision of railway transport services, separation of accounts being compulsory and organisational or institutional separation being optional'. The provider of the track would charge train operators a fee for the use of their track, giving scope for 'open access', under which provision the Wrexham and Shropshire service to Marylebone was operated.

The Railways Act was passed in 1993 and the wheels were in motion, so to speak. Whether the complex structure it established was appropriate is perhaps outside our scope. Railtrack would own the track, signals and infrastructure, while BR's passenger trains and locomotives transferred to three rolling-stock leasing companies. Train Operating Companies would hire trains, pay Railtrack for use of the infrastructure and operate whatever franchise they had successfully bid for. The structure for freight was different – locomotives and rolling stock would henceforth be owned by one of six freight train operators, three broadly regional and three business sector-based, such as Freightliner.

Central Trains: 170 505 arrives at Albrighton, on the Shrewsbury to Wolverhampton line, with a stopping train on 9 June 2007.

At first, twenty-five 'shadow franchises' were created. They were operated by public-sector Train Operating Companies, until the franchises had been put to tender and taken on by their new owners. Provincial had been rebranded Regional Railways in 1989 and its Central division became Central Trains. The franchise was won by National Express Group in 1997, the bright-green liveried trains of which would be a familiar sight until 2007, when the franchise was gained by London Midland. Meanwhile there had been major changes further west – London Midland's only services in Shropshire are the 'locals' on the Shrewsbury to Wolverhampton line.

The changes elsewhere in the county were the result of the creation of the Wales and Borders franchise, announced in 2000. Over the course of the next few years, most services operating in Wales were taken into the franchise, including those running on the former North and West, the only railway connecting North and South Wales. A fifteen-year franchise was awarded to Arriva in 2003 and responsibility for the franchise passed to the Welsh Government later in the decade.

As a result, other than the London Midland trains from Birmingham, all passenger services in Shropshire are currently provided by Arriva Trains Wales, which also manages all the stations apart from those on the Wolverhampton line. With services extending to Manchester and Birmingham International as well as Welsh destinations, the county is well served. Arriva's involvement has not been entirely free of controversy – it has been owned by Deutsche Bahn since 2010.

In the earlier days of privatization, there were some interesting developments. Some shorter services were combined to provide through trains between quite distant locations – there were those who described Central Trains as the 'Barmouth to Yarmouth' railway. The possible benefits to passengers of such services may have been outweighed by their vulnerability to delays. At the other end of the scale, Wellington's bay platform became the terminus, for a few years, of a local service running to Walsall. On the face of it, a good idea, but in practice it may have lost the railway some

passenger traffic. Like some local services in 1922, passengers from Oakengates, Shifnal, Cosford and Albrighton wishing to go to Shrewsbury had to change at Wellington. The service ended in 2006 and today London Midland's local trains run between Birmingham New Street and Shrewsbury, in addition to Arriva's limited stop services from Birmingham International. Services have since settled into a fairly straightforward pattern (examined below), though there will doubtless be further changes. Much work has taken place recently on the Aberystwyth line, with a view to introducing an hourly service. When, or if, that service is implemented, there will inevitably be knock-on effects to other services.

The London Trains

BR's London services of the late 1980s did not last – they ended before privatization. On 10 April 1992, 86 247 *Abraham Darby* pulled the last Shrewsbury-bound service from London Euston. It could not haul it all the way, of course, and as a final reminder of the inconvenience of the service from the operator's standpoint, diesel 47 590 *Thomas Telford* hauled the last leg from Wolverhampton.

In 1997, the InterCity West Coast franchise was awarded to Richard Branson's Virgin Rail Group. The following year, on 25 May, a through London service was introduced. Leaving the county town at 06.48, it was scheduled to arrive at London Euston at 09.51. The return working left at 18.15, arriving in Shrewsbury at 21.04. The first train out was hauled by Virgin-liveried 47822, which was formally named *Pride of Shrewsbury* at Shrewsbury station prior to departure. The service lasted barely three years.

Under the open-access provision, a completely new London service started on 28 April 2008. The 'Wrexham and Shropshire' (W&S) trains ran on the former GWR line via Banbury and Princes Risborough, and the old Great Central's line from Northolt Junction to London's Marylebone station. Because of the existing contract between Virgin Trains and Network Rail, W&S trains could not pick up (southbound) or set down (northbound) at Wolverhampton, nor could they serve Birmingham New Street. Instead, Tame Bridge Parkway would be the only fully served intermediate stop between Shropshire and the capital. Because of the routes available and the need to work with existing services, the trains were not particularly fast. In December 2008, Virgin Trains introduced a through service from Wrexham, via Chester, to London Euston. The 07.00 from Wrexham arrives in London at 09.41; the W&S train took more than four hours.

Throughout its life, the service was operated using locomotives and hauled coaching stock. Maybe not the operator's first choice, they nevertheless provided a high standard of comfort. The spring 2010 National Passenger Survey recorded a satisfaction rating of 99 per cent (the highest recorded by the survey). The service was clearly appreciated by its passengers – but there were never enough of them, despite very competitive fares. Ineligible for public subsidy, the service could not be made profitable. The five trains per day from Wrexham were gradually cut back to three, then, in late January 2011 came the announcement that the service was to be withdrawn from the 28th of that month.

Demise of the Wrexham and Shropshire: the last train to London was the 13.28 from Wrexham. Hauled by 67013 Dyfrbont Pontcysyllte *and strengthened to five coaches, it has just left Shrewsbury, passing Abbey Foregate box on its journey south; 28 January 2012.* STEVE PRICE

The following year, the situation changed yet again. Virgin's fifteen-year franchise for the West Coast services, awarded in 1997, was up for renewal. The outcome of the bidding process, announced in August 2012, was that the franchise would be awarded to First Group. The controversy that followed became national headline news; subsequent analysis revealed flaws in the process and Virgin's franchise was extended – in March 2013 the Government announced that it would run until April 2017.

Given that First Group had stated its intention to reinstate Shrewsbury's London service, Salopians' joy was thus short-lived. Hope was renewed early in 2013 when Virgin Trains announced plans for two trains per day, each way, between Shrewsbury and London. Calling at Wellington and Telford Central, they would then use the Oxley Chord at Wolverhampton to run non-stop to Stafford. The 125mph (200km/h) five-car diesel Class 221 Super Voyager would then reverse to travel up the Trent Valley main line, making one further call at Rugby before arriving in London Euston, two hours and twelve minutes after leaving Shrewsbury. It had been hoped that the service would be in operation by the end of 2013, but Network Rail is concerned that there is not sufficient capacity on the main line for two more trains. The saga will undoubtedly run on …

The proposed route via Stafford is an interesting reflection of the very earliest days of Shropshire's railway, when the Wellington to Stafford line saw the county's first reasonably direct services to the capital, and has revived campaigns to reopen that line. Sadly, that would seem to be unlikely, as would the prospect of electrifying the Shrewsbury to Wolverhampton line, welcome as both might be.

Passenger Services Today

Shrewsbury station remains an important railway centre – it was the origin or destination for 1.7 million passengers in the year 2011/12, plus a further 200,000 changed trains there. All services are operated by modern diesel units, apart from the Premier Service. This locomotive-hauled train runs each weekday between Holyhead and Cardiff, taking just four hours and seventeen minutes for the southbound run. Sponsored by the Welsh Government, it offers first class and dining facilities. As there are no through rail routes within Wales linking North and South, it runs through the Marches, with only three stops – at Chester, Shrewsbury and Hereford – outside the Principality.

By comparison with earlier years, today's timetables are more readily available (via an internet connection) and much clearer (both in terms of the nature of the information and its legibility). Real-time information is available online and at every railway station. Though most of Shropshire's nineteen stations are unstaffed, intending passengers can see at a glance when the next two or three trains are expected, whether they are on time and where they are going.

Loco-hauled express passenger on the North and West: the northbound Arriva Premier Service, with 67002 at the head, arrives at Shrewsbury on 27 June 2012. ROBERT SMOUT

The intensity of the service on most lines is striking. The Wolverhampton line sees the greatest frequency – the December 2012 to May 2013 timetable shows no fewer than thirty-eight westbound trains calling at Telford Central every weekday. Hourly stopping trains between New Street and Shrewsbury are provided by London Midland, while Arriva Trains Wales provides the fast service. Its hourly trains from Birmingham International call at just Telford Central and Wellington after Wolverhampton. From Shrewsbury they then depart alternately to Chester and Holyhead, or to Aberystwyth, providing a two-hourly service to the latter.

Telford Central, which opened on 12 May 1986, topped the one-million passengers mark in 2011/12, whilst Wellington served more than half a million in the same period. They are the county's second and third most used stations. With a journey time of just thirty-five minutes for most express services from Telford Central to Birmingham, it is perhaps not surprising that the station has been hugely successful.

Ludlow, on the Shrewsbury–Hereford line, is the county's fourth busiest station. Twenty-six trains call, in each direction, between 06.00 and midnight on weekdays (the Premier Service passes through at speed ...). Most of these trains constitute the hourly service between Cardiff and Manchester Piccadilly. The great majority originate further

The station building at Oakengates is now used by a dental practice – the recent extension, partly obscured behind the footbridge, could almost be mistaken for a signal box. London Midland 170 514 calls with an eastbound local on 4 June 2013.

175 105 arrives at Gobowen with a Holyhead to Cardiff Central working on 19 February 2013. The train is modern; the small white building on the platform dates from the earliest days of Shropshire's railways.

The view north from Sutton Bridge Junction has changed greatly since steam days, yet remains recognizable. The locomotive shed and the Severn Valley line have gone, but Coleham yard remains, in the form of permanent way sidings and a depot for the locomotives used in conjunction with the Cambrian signalling project. One is seen in the background as 175 108 passes with a Cardiff-bound train on 7 June 2013.

The fourth busiest station in Shropshire in 2011/12, Ludlow's facilities have been improved in recent years. Two three-car Class 175 units depart for the north; the front of the train is passing the former railway goods shed, now home of the Ludlow Brewing Co.; 5 November 2012.

Single-car 153303 is sufficient for the stopping service at Wem on 29 November 2012. Modern shelters now cater for waiting passengers and the days of its signal box are numbered.

west, at Carmarthen, and six start out from Milford Haven. In addition to the Manchester service, there is a Cardiff–Holyhead service. Such trains follow the former GWR route from Shrewsbury to Chester, reversing there to continue their journey.

The Sunday service starts a little later in the day – Ludlow's first northbound train calls at 10.06. It is the first of fifteen northbound trains to call; there were just two in 1922.

The fifth busiest station in Shropshire is Gobowen, the only remaining station within the county on the Chester line. Gobowen receives an hourly service, with trains running alternately between Cardiff and Holyhead, and Birmingham International and Holyhead.

The hourly Cardiff to Manchester trains run between Shrewsbury and Crewe. Most, but not all, call at Whitchurch (eighth busiest station) and a small number also serve Wem; however, all stations on the line (Yorton, Wem, Prees and Whitchurch, within the county) are also served by the Shrewsbury to Crewe stopping train, roughly every two hours. The unstaffed station at

Arriva 170 155 is not stopping at Whitchurch; a small forest grows up against the opposite face of the island platform once used by trains for the Cambrian network; 29 November 2012.

It could almost be a twenty-first century Colonel Stephens station – Broome, on the Central Wales line, had the distinction of being Shropshire's least-used station in 2011/12; 5 November 2012.

Freight Trains through Shropshire

The working timetable for today's rail services is available on the internet, including real-time updates on the actual progress of each train. It shows, for example, that on Monday, 13 May 2013, thirteen paths were provided through Church Stretton for freight trains (though not all of them would run). Their loads are heavy (up to 2,200 tonnes), their origins and destinations are varied and sometimes distant: Westbury (Wilts); Margam (South Wales); Portbury (Avonmouth); Fiddlers Ferry (Merseyside); Carlisle; and Mossend (Motherwell) on this occasion.

A similar picture emerges for Albrighton, on the Wolverhampton line – some of the above trains will travel this way. Additionally, there are paths for the fuel trains running to and from Ironbridge Power Station. Most freight trains merely pass through the county, though another significant destination lies just over the Welsh border – the Kronospan factory at Chirk. The white plume from the factory's chimney can be seen from many parts of Shropshire. Timber for its 'wood panel products and laminate flooring' arrives by rail; as its siding makes a trailing connection to the up main line, deliveries of timber to the siding must approach from the Wrexham direction. Loaded trains from the Shrewsbury direction continue via Crewe and Chester, but empties will travel directly towards Shrewsbury on their return journeys. Similarly, coal from Portbury to Rugeley Power Station usually runs up the North and West, but the empties return by the former Midland route south of Birmingham.

Freight paths are also provided, not every day, for trains that will 'run as required' to the Donnington terminal. The Ironbridge trains are due to end when the power station closes in 2015. However, it is possible that, by then, a new flow of stone from Bayston Hill Quarry will be helping to keep heavy freight off the county's roads.

Whitchurch is a shadow of its former self in physical terms, but twenty-one northbound trains call there every weekday. The Sunday service is sparse – just five trains.

Four trains leave Shrewsbury each day for the leisurely four-hour run to Swansea via the Central Wales line. Two trains run on Sundays, in each direction. The stations at Bucknell, Hopton Heath and Broome are, in that order, seventeenth, eighteenth and nineteenth in the league table. Broome's wooden platform and simple wooden shelter could be relics of the Colonel Stephens era; they saw just 1,472 passengers begin or end their journeys in 2011/12.

A southbound steel train passes Bayston Hill, hauled by EWS-liveried 60052 Tower Colliery on 24 March 2002. One hundred of these locomotives were built in the last years of British Rail; only around twenty remain in service and they are not often seen in Shropshire today.

The newest locomotives on Shropshire's railways are the unusual-looking Class 70s. The first of these 3,690bhp locomotives arrived from General Electric, in the USA, in 2008. Freightliner 70003 is hauling a Portbury to Rugeley coal train out of the freight loop at Sutton Bridge, Shrewsbury; 11 June 2011. STEVE PRICE

66192 rumbles through the now somewhat basic station at Craven Arms with a southbound steel train on 5 November 2012. It still bears the livery of the English, Welsh and Scottish Railway (EWS), which was acquired by DB Schenker in 2007, and will doubtless carry a new livery before too long.

The new look in Coalbrookdale: GBRf 66 746 crosses the viaduct as it carefully descends towards Ironbridge Power Station with a train of pelletized wood on 15 April 2013.

Shropshire's Signals and Shrewsbury Station

At nationalization, virtually all of Shropshire's signalling was of the mechanical variety. Signal boxes were relatively close to one another – there is a limit to just how much wire can be pulled by the signalman's levers. Fewer boxes would reduce the capacity of the lines they controlled – but the number did diminish over the years as services and the need for capacity dwindled.

The usual alternative is the electrically operated colour-light signal, capable of replacing the home (red/green) and distant (yellow) signals and much more. Their adoption within the county has been relatively slow, but has spread inexorably. Outside Shrewsbury, the signal boxes have been disappearing and the semaphore signals replaced by their modern replacements. The Wolverhampton line is now signalled from Saltley, Birmingham, and modern signalling is due to be implemented on the Crewe line during 2013. Boxes remain at present in the Hereford and Chester directions, albeit with some colour-light signals to extend their reach beyond the signalman's 'pull'.

The Cambrian has undergone a more radical signalling solution – twice! Its needs are different from the double-track lines – signalling must be efficient to make the best use of passing loops and to minimize the knock-on delays that any late running may cause. It must also prevent the ultimate horror of the single-track lines, the head-on collision. The notorious disaster near Abermule, between Welshpool and Newtown, in 1921 was one of the worst of its kind.

Its primary cause was that the crew were mistakenly given back the token they had just handed in for the previous stretch of track and failed to check it. Single lines have historically relied on the 'token', in effect a key which must be held by the train crew before proceeding along a stretch of single-line railway. They are still used extensively, both by Network Rail and the preserved railways. However, during the 1980s, an electronic system using radio transmission of unique microprocessor codes was successfully trialled and installed in Scotland, on the Dingwall to Kyle of Lochalsh line. RETB, or Radio Electronic Token Block, was soon extended to other Scottish lines, to the East Suffolk line and to the Cambrian.

The system was undoubtedly successful, but the technology has since been rendered obsolete; in 2006, Network Rail decided to pilot the newest system, ERTMS, on the Cambrian lines. The European Rail Traffic Management System provides automatic train protection using radio transmission of data and voice communication between track and train. As its name suggests, it is seen as a system to be employed across Europe, enabling trains to run across international borders

This signal on platform 7 at Shrewsbury would be unusual even if its arms were the right way up. It originally had smaller 'calling-on' arms below the main arms; 30 June 2013.

Now the biggest mechanical signal box in the world, the length of Severn Bridge Junction's 180-lever frame can be appreciated in this 1987 view. SHROPSHIRE RAILWAY SOCIETY

virtually all of the country's 800 remaining 'traditional' signal boxes over the next fifteen years. Their function will be replaced by just twelve Rail Operating Centres. Once in operation, they will switch from conventional signalling systems to a traffic-management system, which will use internet technologies to interface with signals and associated systems. The days of semaphore signalling will be at an end.

Shrewsbury's Severn Bridge Junction signal box is now the largest remaining mechanical signal box in the world. The previous biggest, in Melbourne, Australia, was replaced by a modern electronic system in 2008. Dating from the major station rebuild in the early years of the twentieth century, the box opened in 1904, to replace a box that stood over the lines above the river. It was constructed to LNWR design, as a joint venture with the GWR. Half of its 180 levers remain in use and it is staffed twenty-four hours a day by two signallers who control an average of 300 train movements per day.

Severn Bridge Junction deals with traffic at the southern end of the station, including the Abbey Foregate loop. It 'talks' to three other mechanical boxes. A little further east is the GWR Abbey Foregate box, taking traffic from the Wolverhampton line. To the south, Sutton Bridge Junction handles traffic for Hereford and the Cambrian lines. At the north end of the station, Crewe Junction performs the function implied by its name. Like Severn Bridge Junction, it is a listed building and is of similar design, but with fewer (120) levers.

without needing to be equipped for country-specific signalling. In the words of Network Rail, 'this European tried and tested system will replace traditional railway signals with a computer display inside every train cab, reducing the costs of maintaining the railway, improving performance and enhancing safety'.

After some testing, ERTMS was brought into full use on the Shrewsbury to Aberystwyth and Pwllheli lines in March 2011. Its deployment means that trains cannot run on those lines unless they are equipped for ERTMS; the cost of the equipment brought to an end several years of steam-hauled excursions along the Cambrian coast.

An article in the July 2013 issue of the *Railway Magazine* describes Network Rail's plans to replace

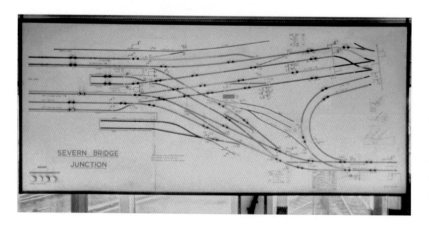

The signaller's diagram inside Severn Bridge Junction box, showing the Abbey curve and the complexity of the layout at the southern end of the station, as it was in 1987. SHROPSHIRE RAILWAY SOCIETY

The semaphores came under threat in the 1980s – the work to replace them was planned, with associated track rationalization, for 1986–7, but never took place. Given the growth in traffic since, it is likely that the rationalized layout would now be a bottleneck. Shrewsbury is thought to be low on Network Rail's 'to do' list, but when the inevitable does happen, the historic value of Severn Bridge Junction should ensure its preservation.

The station's overall roof may have gone more than fifty years ago and there are fewer platforms in use, but Shrewsbury has suffered less than most similar-sized towns. Visitors arriving by rail may appreciate the 'traditional' well-maintained platforms and structures. Shrewsbury has long been denied city status, but its station makes a statement – this is more than just a small provincial town.

Travellers arriving at the station from the town have a very different view. The platforms are out of sight behind the fine and very substantial stone-built frontage which makes the same statement. As it did more than 100 years ago, Shrewsbury station stands gateway to a wide range of destinations near and far – although not London.

Looking back from the south end of Shrewsbury's platform 7: Class 158s are in charge on a quiet Sunday, 30 June 2013. Behind them can be seen the Dana Footbridge and the tower above the main entrance.

Past, Present ... and Future

The timeline of railways in Shropshire extends back more than 400 years, longer than almost anywhere else in the British Isles, or indeed the world. It has been a fascinating, and at times precarious history. The routes followed by today's trains have been in place for more than 150 years, but the trains and the services they operate are vastly different from those of the past, carrying more passengers than ever before. Perhaps by the time this book is in print, the London trains will be running again – taking less than two hours from Telford, a town which did not exist when the GWR's trains ran to Paddington.

The branch-line, steam-powered past is superbly represented by the Severn Valley Railway and remnants of the pre-railway age tramways and wagonways are well cared for by the Ironbridge Gorge Museum. We will hope that the future for the main lines is bright – lit perhaps by sparks from the pantograph of a London-bound electric train in Shrewsbury station …

Finale: as a reminder of earlier times, 5690 Leander heads south near Stokesay with a Welsh Marches Pullman on 13 March 1982.

Selected Further Reading and Bibliography

Baxter, B., *Stone Blocks and Iron Rails* (David and Charles, 1966)

Beddoes, K. and Smith, W., *The Tenbury and Bewdley Railway* (Wild Swan Publications, 1995)

Bolger, P., *BR Steam Motive Power Depots WR* (Ian Allan, 1998)

Bridges, A., *Industrial Locomotives of Cheshire Shropshire and Herefordshire* (Industrial Railway Society, 1977)

Brown, I., *The Mines of Shropshire* (Moorland Publishing Company, 1976)

Christiansen, R., *A Regional History of the Railways of Great Britain: Vol. 13 Thames and Severn* (David and Charles, 1981)

Christiansen, R., *A Regional History of the Railways of Great Britain: Vol. 7 The West Midlands*, 3rd edn (David and Charles, 1991)

Christiansen, R., *Forgotten Railways: North and Mid Wales* (David and Charles, 1984)

Christiansen, R., *Forgotten Railways: Vol. 11 Severn Valley and Welsh Border* (David and Charles, 1988)

Christiansen, R., *Forgotten Railways: Vol. 10 The West Midlands* (David and Charles, 1985)

Conolly, P., *British Railways Pre-Grouping Atlas and Gazetteer* (Ian Allan, 1976)

Griffith, E., *The Bishop's Castle Railway* (Kingfisher Railway Productions, 1983)

Hodge, J., *The North & West Route: Vol. 1 Shrewsbury* (Wild Swan Publications, 2007)

Industrial Railway Society *Industrial Locomotives* (IRS, editions 1EL 1969 – 16EL, 2012)

Johnson, P., *An Illustrated History of the Shropshire and Montgomeryshire Light Railway* (Ian Allan, 2008)

Jones, K., *The Wenlock Branch* (Oakwood Press, 1998)

Jowett, A., *Jowett's Railway Atlas* (Patrick Stephens Ltd, 1989)

Jowett, A., *Jowett's Railway Centres* (Patrick Stephens Ltd, 1993)

Kay, P., *Signalling Atlas and Signal Box Directory, Great Britain and Ireland* (Peter Kay, 1997)

Lloyd, M., *The Tanat Valley Light Railway* (Wild Swan Publications, 1990)

Mitchell, V. and Smith, K., *Craven Arms to Wellington* (Middleton Press, 2008)

Morriss, R., *Rail Centres: Shrewsbury* (Ian Allan, 1986)

Morriss, R., *Railways of Shropshire* (Shropshire Books, 1991)

Pearce, A., *Mining in Shropshire* (Shropshire Books, 1995)

Price, M., *The Cleobury Mortimer and Ditton Priors Light Railway* (Oakwood Press, 1995)

Rhodes, N., *Trains on the Border – The Railways of Llanymynech and Pant* (Neil Rhodes Books, 2012)

Rolt, T., *Red for Danger* (Pan Books, 1978)

Savage, R. and Smith, L., *The Waggon-ways and Plateways of East Shropshire* (Birmingham School of Architecture, 1965)

Smith, W. and Beddoes, K., *The Cleobury Mortimer and Ditton Priors Light Railway* (Oxford Publishing Co.,1980)

Thomas, C., *Quarry Hunslets of North Wales* (Oakwood Press, 2001)

Tonks, E., *The Shropshire and Montgomeryshire Railway* (Industrial Railway Society, 2007)

Vanns, M., *Severn Valley Railway – A View from the Past* (Ian Allan, 1998)

Yate, R., *By Great Western to Crewe* (Oakwood Press, 2005)

Yate, R., *The Railways and Locomotives of the Lilleshall Company* (Irwell Press, 2008)

Yate, R., *The Shropshire Union Railway* (Oakwood Press, 2003)

Index